2

Contemporary Topics

21st Century Skills for Academic Success

FOURTH EDITION

Ellen Kisslinger

Jeanette Clement
Cynthia Lennox
CONTRIBUTING AUTHORS

Michael Rost
SERIES EDITOR

***Contemporary Topics 2*, High Intermediate**
21st Century Skills for Academic Success
Fourth Edition

Pearson Education, 221 River Street, Hoboken, NJ 07030

Staff credits: The people who made up the ***Contemporary Topics*** team, representing editorial, production, design, and manufacturing, are Pietro Alongi, Claire Bowers, Stephanie Bullard, Kim Casey, Tracey Cataldo, Mindy DePalma, Dave Dickey, Pam Fishman, Niki Lee, Fabrizio Luccitti, Amy McCormick, Jennifer Raspiller, Robert Ruvo, Leigh Stolle, Paula Van Ells, and Joseph Vella.

Cover image: © Fotolia/Suchota
Text composition: MPS North America
Photo credits: See page 134

Library of Congress Cataloging-in-Publication Data
A catalog record for the print edition is available from the Library of Congress
ISBN-10: 0-13-440080-1   ISBN-13: 978-0-13-440080-8

Printed in the United States of America.
4   17

Contents

Scope and Sequence

UNIT SUBJECT AND TITLE	CORPUS-BASED VOCABULARY	NOTE-TAKING AND LISTENING FOCUS	PRONUNCIATION	DISCUSSION STRATEGY	PRESENTATION
1 **SOCIOLOGY** Names	assignment classic discrimination gender generation image neutral prime symbol	Main ideas	Syllable stress	• **Asking for clarification or confirmation** • Asking for opinions or ideas	Present on names, using an outline
2 **LINGUISTICS** Global English	acknowledge communicate domain facilitate global nevertheless retain unprecedented	Comparisons	Stressing words to focus the listener	• **Disagreeing** • Agreeing	Present on varieties of English, using examples
3 **PSYCHOLOGY** Phobias	constant duration physical psychologist rational	Key words	Contractions	• **Keeping a discussion on topic** • Asking for clarification or confirmation • Offering a fact or example	Present on overcoming a fear, using descriptive sensory details
4 **BUSINESS** Success in the Global Economy	acquire adapt attribute complex consumer diverse illustrate	Topics and subtopics	Reduced vowels	• **Trying to reach a consensus** • Asking for clarification or confirmation • Paraphrasing	Present on a formula for success after developing an introduction
5 **EDUCATION** How We Each Learn Best	accurately assess aware demonstrate logic mental notion option	Numbered lists	Final -s and -ed sounds	• **Expressing an opinion** • Asking for clarification or confirmation • Offering a fact or example	Present on learning strengths, using transitions
6 **HISTORY** The Silk Road	alternate conflict decade decline network route	Dates and numbers	Thought groups	• **Paraphrasing** • Asking for opinions or ideas • Offering a fact or example	Present on an impactful person, using a conclusion

UNIT SUBJECT AND TITLE	CORPUS-BASED VOCABULARY	NOTE-TAKING AND LISTENING FOCUS	PRONUNCIATION	DISCUSSION STRATEGY	PRESENTATION
7 SOCIAL PSYCHOLOGY Sports Fans	appreciate bond commitment display integral motivate ongoing reinforce	Enumerating	Linked sounds	▪ **Agreeing** ▪ Asking for clarification or confirmation ▪ Asking for opinions or ideas	Present on a special passion, using an attention-getting opener
8 ARCHITECTURE Frank Gehry	dynamic foundation objective principle stress utilize	Emphasis	Intonation	▪ **Acknowledging a point** ▪ Asking for opinions or ideas ▪ Disagreeing	Present on a beautiful building, using visual aids
9 PUBLIC HEALTH Global Epidemic	approximately contribute guidelines implement negative shift	Symbols and abbreviations	Emphasized words	▪ **Offering a fact or example** ▪ Asking for opinions or ideas ▪ Paraphrasing	Present on healthy changes, using nonverbal communication
10 URBAN PLANNING 21st Century Cities	ethnic expand fundamental initiate institute monitor project	Connected ideas	Reduced and contracted words	▪ **Focusing on a topic** ▪ Asking for clarification or confirmation ▪ Expressing an opinion	Present on a great place to live while persuading the audience
11 BIOLOGY DNA Testing	access concentrate extract identical medical reveal statistically	Graphic organizers	Stressing words to make ideas clear	▪ **Getting a discussion started** ▪ Disagreeing ▪ Expressing an opinion	Present on a scientific advance, using quotations
12 PUBLIC ADMINISTRATION Risk Management	allocate cooperate ignore minimize predict priorities target ultimately widespread	Questions	Key words in thought groups	▪ **Asking for opinions or ideas** ▪ Agreeing ▪ Offering a fact or example	Present on a survivor's story and answer audience questions

Acknowledgments

The series editor, authors, and publisher would like to thank the following consultants, reviewers, and teachers for offering their invaluable insights and suggestions for the fourth edition of the *Contemporary Topics* series.

Kate Reynolds, *University of Wisconsin-Eau Claire*; Kathie Gerecke, *North Shore Community College*; Jeanne Dunnett, *Central Connecticut State University*; Linda Anderson, *Washington University in St. Louis/Fontbonne University*; Sande Wu, *California State University, Fresno*; Stephanie Landon, *College of the Desert*; Jungsook Kim, *Jeungsang Language School*; Jenny Oh Kim, *Kangnamgu Daechidong*; Patty Heiser, *University of Washington*; Carrie Barnard, *Queens College*; Lori D. Giles, *University of Miami*; Nancy H. Centers, *Roger Williams University*; Lyra Riabov, *Southern New Hampshire University*; Dr. Steven Gras, *ESL Program, SUNY Plattsburgh*; series consultants Jeanette Clement and Cynthia Lennox, *Duquesne University*

The author would also like to thank Rachel Belanger and Jennifer Bixby for their valuable contributions as well the many people at Pearson, in particular Amy McCormick, for their dedication to the series. I would also like to thank Michael Rost, with whom I've shared the challenge of addressing the needs of our students in academic listening for many years. His keen insight regarding the complexity of skills needed by students to support their success academically has made the series possible.

New to this fourth edition, **Essential Online Resources** are available at **www.pearsonelt.com/ contemporarytopics4e**, using your access code. These resources include the following:

- **VIDEO:** Watch the Lecture academic lecture videos, with or without Presentation Points, and Talk About the Topic student discussion videos are available.
- **AUDIO:** Audio clips for all audio-based Student Book activities as well as Unit Tests and Proficiency Assessment lectures are available. Audio versions of the unit lectures and student discussion are also provided. (Audio and video icons in the Student Book and Teaching Tips indicate which media is needed for each activity.)
- **STUDENT BOOK PRESENTATION SLIDES:** All units of the Student Book are available as PowerPoint® slides, allowing activities to be viewed as a class.
- **INTERACTIVE TESTS:** Teachers can administer the Unit Tests and Proficiency Assessments online.
- **PRINT RESOURCES:** Transcripts of the videos and lecture-specific Coaching Tips (covering listening, critical thinking, and note-taking) are provided along with Teaching Tips, Answer Keys, Audioscripts, Teacher and Student Evaluations Forms, Unit Tests, and Proficiency Assessments.

Introduction

The *Contemporary Topics* series provides a comprehensive approach to developing 21st century academic skills—including listening, thinking, discussion, presentation, and study skills—in order to prepare students for participation in real-life academic and professional contexts.

The overriding principle of language and skill development in the *Contemporary Topics* series is *engagement*. Activities in each unit are carefully sequenced in a way that gives students increasing involvement and self-direction of their learning. Authentic, stimulating content is introduced and developed throughout each unit so that students experience the value of understanding and exchanging contemporary ideas in a range of academic fields. *Contemporary Topics* is intended to bridge the gap between language-focused and content-focused instruction, to ready students for genuine academic and professional contexts where they will be expected to participate fully.

Each unit centers around a short academic lecture. Realistic preparation activities, focused listening tasks, personalized discussions, challenging tests, and authentic presentation assignments enable students to explore each topic deeply.

The lecture topics are drawn from a range of academic disciplines, and the lectures themselves feature engaging instructors in a variety of settings including offices, lecture halls, and classrooms, many with live student audiences.

In order to achieve the goals of content-based instruction, the *Contemporary Topics* series has developed an engaging nine-part learning methodology:

Section 1: Connect to the Topic

Estimated time: 15 minutes

This opening section invites students to activate what they already know about the unit topic by connecting the topic to their personal experiences and beliefs. Typically, students fill out a short survey and compare answers with a partner. The students then listen to a short interview providing one expert view on the unit topic. The teacher then acts as a facilitator for students to share some of their initial ideas about the topic before they explore it further.

Section 2: Build Your Vocabulary

Estimated time: 15 minutes

This section familiarizes students with some of the key content words and phrases used in the lecture. Each lecture targets 10–15 key words from the Academic Word List to ensure that students learn the core vocabulary needed for academic success.

Students read *and listen* to the target words and phrases in context so that they can better prepare for the upcoming lecture. Students then work individually or with a partner to complete exercises to ensure an initial understanding of the target lexis of the unit. A supplementary pair-work activity enables students to focus on form as they are learning new words and collocations.

Section 3: Focus Your Attention

Estimated time: 10 minutes

In this section, students learn strategies for listening actively and taking clear notes. Because a major part of "active listening" involves a readiness to deal with comprehension difficulties, this section provides specific coaching tips to help students direct their attention and gain more control of how they listen.

Tips include how to use signal words as organization cues, make lists, note definitions, link examples to main ideas, identify causes and effects, and separate points of view. A Try It section, based on a short audio extract, allows students to work on note-taking strategies before they get to the main lecture. Examples of actual notes are usually provided in this section to give students concrete "starter models" they can use in the classroom.

Section 4: Watch the Lecture

Estimated time: 20–30 minutes

As the central section of each unit, Watch the Lecture allows for two full listening cycles, one to focus on "top-down listening" strategies (Listen for Main Ideas) and one to focus on "bottom-up listening" strategies (Listen for Details).

In keeping with the principles of content-based instruction, students are provided with several layers of support. In the Think About It section, students are guided to activate concepts and vocabulary they have studied earlier in the unit.

The lecture can be viewed as a video or just listened to on audio. The video version includes the speaker's Presentation Points.

Section 5: Hear the Language

Estimated time: 10 minutes

This section focuses on "bottom-up" listening strategies and pronunciation. In this section, students hear ten short extracts taken from the actual lecture and perform a noticing task. The task helps students perceive sound reductions and assimilations, learn to hear language as "thought groups" and pauses, and tune in to function of stress and intonation.

Students then work in pairs to practice their pronunciation, adapting the phonology point that was learned in the listening task.

Section 6: Talk About the Topic

Estimated time: 15 minutes

Here students gain valuable discussion skills as they talk about the content of the lectures. Discussion skills are an important part of academic success, and most students benefit from structured practice with these skills. In this activity, students first listen to a short "model discussion" involving native and nonnative speakers, and identify the speaking strategies and gambits that are used. They then attempt to use some of those strategies in their own discussion groups.

The discussion strategies modeled and explained across the units include the following:

- Agreeing
- Asking for clarification or confirmation
- Asking for opinions or ideas
- Disagreeing
- Expressing an opinion

- Keeping a discussion on topic
- Offering a fact or example
- Trying to reach a consensus
- Paraphrasing

Section 7: Review Your Notes

Estimated time: 10 minutes

Using notes for review and discussion is an important study skill that is developed in this section. Research has shown that the value of note-taking for memory building is realized *primarily* when note-takers review their notes and attempt to reconstruct the content.

In this activity, students are guided in reviewing the content of the unit, clarifying concepts, and preparing for the Unit Test. Abbreviated examples of actual notes are provided to help students compare and improve their own note-taking skills.

Section 8: Take the Unit Test and Proficiency Assessment

Estimated time: 15 minutes each

Taking the **Unit Test** completes the study cycle of the unit: preparation for the lecture, listening to the lecture, review of the content, and assessment.

The Unit Test, contained only in the Teacher's Pack, is administered by the teacher and then completed in class, using the accompanying audio. The tests in *Contemporary Topics* are intended to be challenging—to motivate students to learn the material thoroughly. The format features an answer sheet with choices. The question "stem" is provided on audio only. Test-taking skills include verbatim recall, paraphrasing, inferencing, and synthesizing information from different parts of the lecture.

The **Proficiency Assessment** is an audio lecture and ten multiple-choice questions designed to give students practice listening and taking standardized tests. It, too, is found only in the Teacher's Pack and should be administered by the teacher and completed in class using the accompanying audio.

Section 9: Express Your Ideas

Estimated time: Will vary by class size

This final section creates a natural extension of the unit topic to areas that are relevant to students. Students go through a guided process of preparing, practicing, and presenting on a topic of personal interest. Students are also given guidance in listening to other students' presentations and providing helpful feedback.

A supplementary Teacher's Pack (TP) contains teaching tips, transcripts, answer keys, tests, and teacher evaluation forms.

We hope you will enjoy using this course. While the *Contemporary Topics* series provides an abundance of learning activities and media, the key to making the course work in your classroom is student engagement and commitment. For content-based learning to be effective, students need to become *active* learners. This involves thinking critically, guessing, interacting, offering ideas, collaborating, questioning, and responding. The authors and editors of *Contemporary Topics* have created a rich framework for encouraging students to become active, successful learners. We hope that we have also provided you, the teacher, with tools for becoming an active guide to the students in their learning.

Michael Rost
SERIES EDITOR

Learning Path

ACTIVATION SECTIONS 1 / 2 / 3

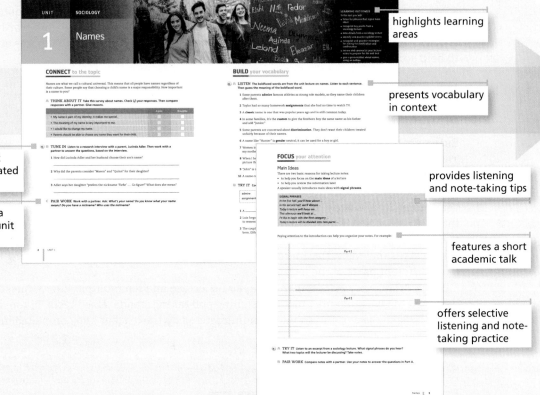

highlights learning areas

presents vocabulary in context

features a short "interview" related to unit theme

encourages idea sharing about unit topic

provides listening and note-taking tips

features a short academic talk

offers selective listening and note-taking practice

EXPRESSION SECTION 9

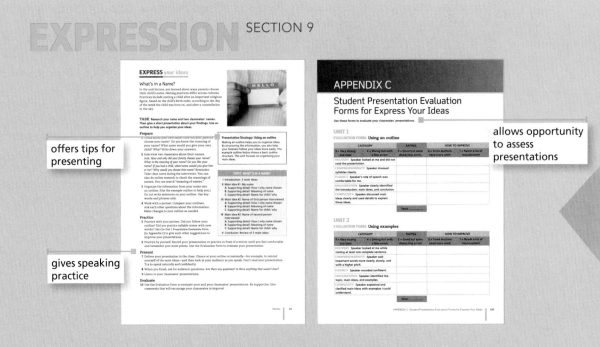

offers tips for presenting

gives speaking practice

allows opportunity to assess presentations

PROCESSING SECTIONS 4 / 5 / 6

encourages anticipation of lecture topic

features an academic lecture and requires gist and intensive listening, and active note-taking

features lecture extracts that demonstrate phonology points

prompts pronunciation practice

features model discussion and listening target

provides tips for participating in a discussion

provides speaking and listening practice

ASSESSMENT SECTIONS 7 / 8

provides opportunity to revise notes

allows demonstration of content mastery

features a short academic lecture and offers assessment within a high-stakes listening environment

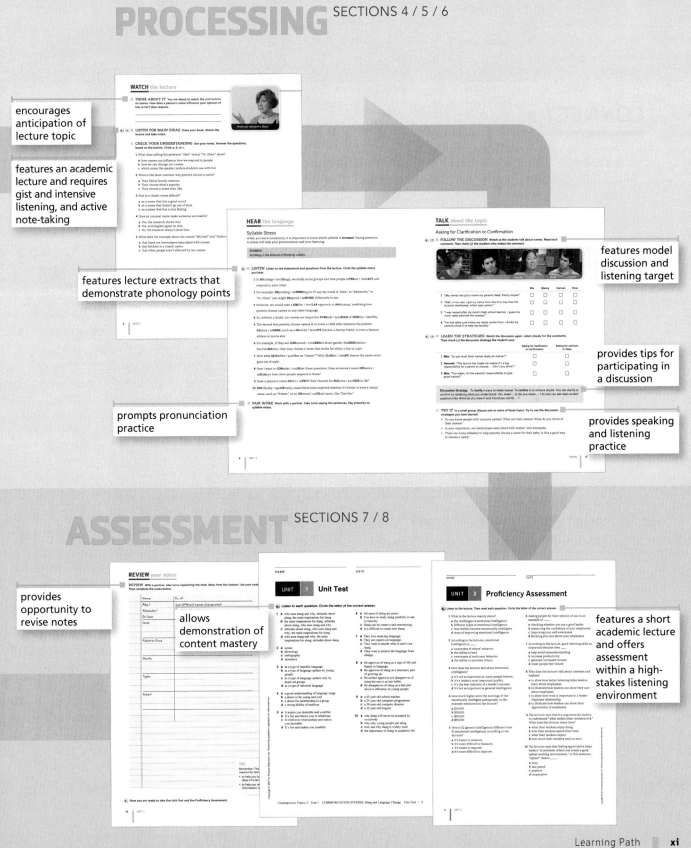

UNIT SOCIOLOGY

1 Names

CONNECT to the topic

Names are what we call a cultural universal. This means that all people have names regardless of their culture. Some people say that choosing a child's name is a major responsibility. How important is a name to you?

A THINK ABOUT IT Take this survey about names. Check (✓) your responses. Then compare responses with a partner. Give reasons.

	Agree	Disagree
• My name is part of my identity; it makes me special.	☐	☐
• The meaning of my name is very important to me.	☐	☐
• I would like to change my name.	☐	☐
• Parents should be able to choose any name they want for their child.	☐	☐

B TUNE IN Listen to a research interview with a parent, Lucinda Adler. Then work with a partner to answer the questions, based on the interview.

1 How did Lucinda Adler and her husband choose their son's name?

_____

2 Why did the parents consider "Mason" and "Quinn" for their daughter?

_____

3 Adler says her daughter "prefers the nickname 'Fiefie' ... . Go figure!" What does she mean?

_____

C PAIR WORK Work with a partner. Ask: *What's your name? Do you know what your name means? Do you have a nickname? Who uses the nickname?*

LEARNING OUTCOMES
In this unit you will:
- listen for phrases that signal main ideas
- recognize key points from a sociology lecture
- note details from a sociology lecture
- identify and practice syllable stress
- recognize and practice strategies for asking for clarification and confirmation
- review and summarize your lecture notes to prepare for the unit test
- give a presentation about names, using an outline

BUILD your vocabulary

A LISTEN The boldfaced words are from the unit lecture on names. Listen to each sentence. Then guess the meaning of the boldfaced word.

1 Some parents **admire** famous athletes as strong role models, so they name their children after them.

2 Taylor had so many homework **assignments** that she had no time to watch TV.

3 A **classic** name is one that was popular years ago and is still common today.

4 In some families, it's the **custom** to give the firstborn boy the same name as his father and add "Junior."

5 Some parents are concerned about **discrimination**. They don't want their children treated unfairly because of their names.

6 A name like "Hunter" is **gender** neutral; it can be used for a boy or girl.

7 Women in three **generations** of my family have had the name "Sarah"—my grandmother, my mother, and my sister.

8 When I hear the name "Barbie," I see an **image** of a tall, blond girl. Fair or not, it's the picture that comes into my mind.

9 "John" is a **prime** example of a classic name. It's been used for many years.

10 A name can be a **symbol** of identity, especially for celebrities.

B TRY IT Complete each sentence with the correct word.

admire	classic	discrimination	generations	prime
assignments	custom	gender	image	symbol

1 A _____ name like *Robert* has been used for a long time.

2 Luis forgot the woman's name although the _____ of her face was easy to remember.

3 The couple didn't want to know the _____ of their baby before it was born. Either a boy or a girl was fine.

4 In my opinion, a(n) _____ example of a bad name is a name that's hard to pronounce.

5 Mr. Lee gave his students three _____ for the weekend.

6 Because the Martins were worried about gender _____ , they gave their daughter a name used by both boys and girls.

7 The _____ in our family is to name a baby after a relative who has recently died.

8 Basketball star Lebron James is called "The King" because of his _____ as the best player in the world.

9 In Robert's family, four _____ have the name "Robert," including Robert's great-grandfather.

10 For their new baby, my neighbors chose the name of a politician they _____ in hopes that their daughter will also be successful.

C **PAIR WORK** Read the sentences with a partner. Notice the boldfaced words. Then choose a particle to complete each sentence.

after	as	by	of	to

1 An **example** _____ an unusual name is "Sky."

2 Unfortunately, people are **judged** _____ the names they have.

3 Steven was **named** _____ his dad's college coach, Mr. Stevens.

4 "Emily" **qualifies** _____ a classic name because it's always been popular.

5 Sociologists study how people **respond** _____ each other's names.

down	on	out of	to	with

6 Stereotypes are **associated** _____ some names. For example, some people expect a "Jennifer" to be pretty.

7 Some couples choose a name in hopes it will provide some social **benefit** _____ their child—for example, their child will be popular or respected.

8 The name "Anna" was **passed** _____ from one generation to the next in the girl's family.

9 Some parents don't **rely** _____ custom. Instead, they choose a name they like.

10 A classic name never goes _____ **style**. It's always popular.

FOCUS your attention

Main Ideas

There are two basic reasons for taking lecture notes:

- to help you focus on the **main ideas** of a lecture
- to help you review the information later

A speaker usually introduces main ideas with **signal phrases**.

SIGNAL PHRASES

*In the first half, **you'll hear about** …*
*In the second half, **we'll discuss** …*
*Today's lecture **will focus on** …*
*This afternoon **we'll look at** …*
*I'd like to begin with **the first category** …*
*Today's lecture will be **divided into two parts:** …*

Paying attention to the introduction can help you organize your notes. For example:

Part 1

Part 2

🔊 **A TRY IT** Listen to an excerpt from a sociology lecture. What signal phrases do you hear? What two topics will the lecturer be discussing? Take notes.

B PAIR WORK Compare notes with a partner. Use your notes to answer the questions in Part A.

WATCH the lecture

A **THINK ABOUT IT** You are about to watch the unit lecture on names. How does a person's name influence your opinion of him or her? Give reasons.

_____

_____

Professor Alexandra Shaw

B **LISTEN FOR MAIN IDEAS** Close your book. Watch the lecture and take notes.

C **CHECK YOUR UNDERSTANDING** Use your notes. Answer the questions, based on the lecture. Circle *a*, *b*, or *c*.

1 What does calling the professor "Alex" versus "Dr. Shaw" show?

   a how names can influence how we respond to people
   b how we can change our names
   c which name the speaker prefers students use with her

2 What is the most common way parents choose a name?

   a They follow family customs.
   b They choose what's popular.
   c They choose a name they like.

3 How is a classic name defined?

   a as a name that has a good sound
   b as a name that doesn't go out of style
   c as a name that has a nice feeling

4 Does an unusual name make someone successful?

   a Yes, the research shows this.
   b Yes, sociologists agree on this.
   c No, the research doesn't show this.

5 What does the example about the names "Michael" and "Hubert" tell us?

   a that there are stereotypes associated with names
   b that Michael is a classic name
   c that other people aren't affected by our names

 **D LISTEN FOR DETAILS** Close your book. Watch the lecture again. Add details to your notes and correct any mistakes.

E CHECK YOUR UNDERSTANDING Use your notes. Decide if the statements are *T* (true) or *F* (false), based on the lecture. Correct any false statements.

_____ **1** A *cultural universal* is defined as a practice we all share.

_____ **2** A first name is also referred to as *a given name*.

_____ **3** In some families, it's custom to name the first son after the grandmother.

_____ **4** "Taylor" is an example of a name that works for either gender.

_____ **5** Some parents believe a name can give their child social benefit.

_____ **6** "Alex" and "Emily" are examples of classic names.

_____ **7** Sociologists agree that it is better to have a classic than an unusual name.

_____ **8** The name "Hubert" was on all of the homework assignments.

_____ **9** The teachers were given the same homework assignment.

_____ **10** Parents who want their son to be considered smart should name him "Hubert."

HEAR the language

Syllable Stress

When you learn vocabulary, it is important to know which syllable is **stressed**. Paying attention to stress will help your pronunciation and your listening.

> **EXAMPLE**
> *SociOlogy is the SCIence of STUdying soCIety.*

A LISTEN Listen to the statements and questions from the lecture. Circle the syllable stress you hear.

1 In **SO**ciology / soci**OL**ogy, we study social groups and how people in**TER**act / inter**ACT** and respond to each other.

2 For example, **DE**pending / de**PEND**ing on if I say my name is "Alex," or "Alexandra," or "Dr. Shaw," you might **RE**spond / re**SPOND** differently to me.

3 However, we would take a **SIM**ilar / simi**LAR** approach to **AN**alyzing / an**A**lizing how parents choose names in any other language.

4 So, without a doubt, our names are important **SYM**bols / sym**BOLS** of i**DEN**tity / iden**TI**ty.

5 The second way parents choose names is to name a child after someone the parents **AD**mire / ad**MIRE**, such as a **FA**vorite / favor**ITE** teacher, a family friend, or even a famous athlete or movie star.

6 For example, if they are **CON**cerned / con**CERN**ed about gender dis**CRIM**ination / discrimi**NA**tion, they may choose a name that works for either a boy or a girl.

7 Now what **QUAL**ifies / qual**I**fies as "classic"? Well, **CLAS**sic / clas**SIC** means the name never goes out of style.

8 Now I want to **CON**sider / con**SI**der these questions: Does someone's name **IN**fluence / in**FLU**ence how other people respond to them?

9 Does a person's name **AF**fect / af**FECT** their chances for **SUC**cess / suc**CESS** in life?

10 **SPE**cifically / spe**CIF**ically, researchers have explored whether it's better to have a classic name, such as "Robert," or an **UN**usual / un**US**ual name, like "Darvlin."

B PAIR WORK Work with a partner. Take turns saying the sentences. Pay attention to syllable stress.

TALK about the topic

Asking for Clarification or Confirmation

A FOLLOW THE DISCUSSION Watch as the students talk about names. Read each comment. Then check (√) the student who makes the comment.

Mia　　Manny　　Hannah　　River

	Mia	Manny	Hannah	River
1 "(My name) was just a name my parents liked. Pretty simple!"	☐	☐	☐	☐
2 "Well, in my case, I got my name from the first way that the lecturer mentioned, which was custom."	☐	☐	☐	☐
3 "I was named after my mom's high school teacher. I guess my mom really admired this woman."	☐	☐	☐	☐
4 "I'm not really sure where my name comes from. I doubt my parents chose it to help me socially."	☐	☐	☐	☐

B LEARN THE STRATEGIES Watch the discussion again. Listen closely for the comments. Then check (√) the discussion strategy the student uses.

	Asking for clarification or confirmation	Asking for opinions or ideas
1 Mia: "So you must think names really *do* matter?"	☐	☐
2 Hannah: "This lecture has made me realize it's a big responsibility for a parent to choose. ... Don't you think?"	☐	☐
3 Mia: "You mean, it's the parents' responsibility to give good names?"	☐	☐

Discussion Strategy　To **clarify** means to make clearer. To **confirm** is to remove doubt. You can clarify or confirm by restating what you understood: *You mean ...* or *Do you mean ... ?* Or you can ask open-ended questions like *What do you mean?* and *Could you clarify ... ?*

C TRY IT In a small group, discuss one or more of these topics. Try to use the discussion strategies you have learned.

- Do you know people with unusual names? What are their names? What do you think of their names?
- In your experience, are stereotypes associated with names? Give examples.
- There are many websites to help parents choose a name for their baby. Is this a good way to choose a name?

REVIEW your notes

REVIEW With a partner, take turns explaining the main ideas from the lecture. Use your notes. Then complete the notes below.

Name:	Ex. of:
Alex /	how different names change what
Alexandra /	we think of people
Dr. Shaw	
Sarah	
Robert or Anna	
Darvlin	
Taylor	
Hubert	

> **TIP!**
> Remember: There are two basic reasons for taking notes:
> • to help you focus on the main ideas of a lecture
> • to help you review information later

🔊 **Now you are ready to take the Unit Test and the Proficiency Assessment.**

EXPRESS your ideas

What's in a Name?

In the unit lecture, you learned about ways parents choose their child's name. Naming practices differ across cultures. Practices include naming a child after an important religious figure, based on the child's birth order, according to the day of the week the child was born on, and after a constellation in the sky.

TASK **Research your name and two classmates' names. Then give a short presentation about your findings. Use an outline to help you organize your ideas.**

Prepare

1 Think about your own name. How did your parents choose your name? Do you know the meaning of your name? What name would you give your own child? Why? Write down your answers.

2 Interview two classmates about their names. Ask: *How and why did your family choose your name? What is the meaning of your name? Do you like your name? If you had a child, what name would you give him or her? Why would you choose this name?* Reminder: Take clear notes during the interviews. You can also do online research to check the meanings of names. You can search "meaning of names."

3 Organize the information from your notes into an outline. (Use the example outline to help you.) Do not write sentences on your outline. Use key words and phrases only.

4 Work with a partner. Compare your outlines. Ask each other questions about the information. Make changes to your outline as needed.

Practice

5 Practice with your partner. Did you follow your outline? Did you practice syllable stress with new words? Use the *Unit 1 Presentation Evaluation Form* (in Appendix C) to give each other suggestions to improve your presentations.

6 Practice by yourself. Record your presentation or practice in front of a mirror until you feel comfortable and remember your main points. Use the Evaluation Form to evaluate your presentation.

Present

7 Deliver your presentation to the class. Glance at your outline occasionally—for example, to remind yourself of the main ideas—and then look at your audience as you speak. Don't read your presentation. Try to speak naturally and confidently.

8 When you finish, ask for audience questions: *Are there any questions? Is there anything that wasn't clear?*

9 Listen to your classmates' presentations.

Evaluate

10 Use the Evaluation Form to evaluate your and your classmates' presentations. Be supportive: Give comments that will encourage your classmates to improve!

Presentation Strategy: Using an outline

Making an outline helps you to organize ideas. By structuring the information, you also help your listeners follow your ideas more easily. The example outline below shows a basic outline structure. This unit focuses on organizing your main ideas.

TOPIC: WHAT'S IN A NAME?

I Introduction: 3 main ideas

II Main idea #1: My name
  A Supporting detail: How / why name chosen
  B Supporting detail: Meaning of name
  C Supporting detail: Name for child / why

III Main idea #2: Name of first person interviewed
  A Supporting detail: How / why name chosen
  B Supporting detail: Meaning of name
  C Supporting detail: Name for child / why

IV Main idea #3: Name of second person interviewed
  A Supporting detail: How / why name chosen
  B Supporting detail: Meaning of name
  C Supporting detail: Name for child / why

V Conclusion: Review of 3 main ideas

---

2 Global English

CONNECT to the topic

Most people would agree that English is the current *lingua franca* of the world—that is, the most commonly used language. On the Internet and in face-to-face situations—at airports, hotels, and business meetings—English is the international language of choice.

A THINK ABOUT IT Consider these questions about using English. Then compare responses with a partner.

- In what situations do you use English now?
- In what future situations might you need English?
- What jobs in your home country require English?
- How often do you speak English with someone whose first language is not English?

B TUNE IN Listen to a job interview with applicant Brian Fisher. Then work with a partner to answer the questions, based on the interview.

1 What position is Brian Fisher interviewing for?

_____

2 What work experience has prepared Fisher for this job?

_____

3 Why does Fisher want this job?

_____

4 Why does the interviewer ask Fisher about challenging situations?

_____

5 Why does Fisher say, "English was valuable for communicating with the guests"?

_____

C PAIR WORK Work with a partner. Ask: *Why do you think English has become the common language globally? Do you ever use English words as you are speaking your first language? If so, in what situations?*

BUILD your vocabulary

A LISTEN The boldfaced words are from the unit lecture on English as a global language. Listen to each sentence. Then guess the meaning of the boldfaced word.

1 Most people **acknowledge** that English is used all over the world. There is very little disagreement about that.

2 In many international situations, people **communicate** in English.

3 English is used widely in certain **domains**, such as business and science.

4 The Portuguese taxi driver and the German tourist used English to **facilitate** communication because it was the only language they both knew.

5 English is considered a **global** language because it's used on every continent.

6 Many people in Japan can speak some English. **Nevertheless**, this doesn't mean English is their primary language; Japanese is.

7 English is one of the **official** languages of the European Union. It's used among EU representatives in major meetings.

8 Because the flight attendant was **proficient** in English, French, and Spanish, he could speak with almost all of the passengers.

9 The hotel employees in Beijing learned English, but of course, **retained** their ability to speak Chinese. Now they use both languages at work.

10 The number of people who currently speak some English is **unprecedented**. More people speak it now than ever before.

B TRY IT Circle the best definition for each boldfaced word.

1 Most people **acknowledge** ...

wish   prefer   accept as true

2 the language used to **communicate** in

share information   call   present

3 used in certain **domains**

organizations	*areas or fields*	*factors*

4 to **facilitate** communication

present	*slow down*	*help make happen*

5 a **global** language

important	*worldwide*	*large*

6 **Nevertheless**, this doesn't mean …

Although true	*In addition*	*Furthermore*

7 one of the **official** languages

correct	*informal*	*approved by an authority*

8 **proficient** in both English and Spanish

productive	*skillful*	*creative*

9 **retained** their ability

kept	*refused*	*lost*

10 the number of people is **unprecedented**

unknown	*unnoticed*	*never happened before*

C PAIR WORK Work with a partner. Notice the boldfaced words. Take turns saying the sentences, ordering the words correctly.

1 The linguistics professor (an / **authority** / is / **on**) the use of English.

2 In the future, (English / **of** / used / be / will / **instead**) other languages like French and Chinese?

3 I know that there are (**view** / **points** / contrasting / two / **of**) about English.

4 Thomas grew up speaking English but (languages / **proficient** / was / four / **in** / other) as well.

5 The idea (is / linguists / **by** / **supported** / many) and is popular.

6 Some contend that other languages won't (be / **replaced** / English / **by**).

7 It's evident that (use / **work** / English / many / **at** / people), but not at home.

8 Will non-English-speaking countries (**hold** / **to** / want / **on** / to) their own languages?

9 I don't believe (an / need / we / that **standard** / **international**) **for** English.

10 Some people, like taxi drivers, may only know (**for** / English / the / **required**) their jobs.

FOCUS your attention

Comparisons

At the beginning of a lecture that compares ideas, a speaker often will say how the lecture is going to be organized.

COMPARISON SIGNAL WORDS

Today you'll hear **two contrasting points of view** about learning English.

This afternoon we'll **compare** American English and British English.

We'll look at some of **the differences between** written and spoken English.

When you hear these signal words, one way to organize your notes is to use two columns to separate the ideas you hear. Say you hear this: *Today I'm going to present **two contrasting points of view** about varieties of English: One view is that it's a problem; the other view is that it isn't. I'm also going to present three supporting arguments for each.* Your notes might look like this:

Varieties of English: A Problem?

A problem	Not a problem
1	1
2	2
3	3

A TRY IT Listen to an excerpt from a talk about varieties of English. What ideas are compared? Take notes.

B PAIR WORK Compare notes with a partner.

WATCH the lecture

Professor Brian Murphy

A THINK ABOUT IT You are about to watch the unit lecture on English as a global language. Do you think English will continue to be the world's *lingua franca*? Think of two reasons to support your answer.

- _____

- _____

B LISTEN FOR MAIN IDEAS Close your book. Watch the lecture and take notes.

C CHECK YOUR UNDERSTANDING Use your notes. Answer the questions, based on the lecture. Circle *a*, *b*, or *c*.

1 What aspect of English as a global language does the speaker mainly discuss?

   a why people like to use English
   b whether English will eventually replace other languages
   c where English is most popular

2 What is the main reason given for the widespread use of English?

   a There are many Internet users.
   b There is a need for a common language.
   c English speakers want everyone to learn English.

3 Why does the speaker mention that English is the dominant language of science and international business?

   a to show that scientists like English
   b to show that a common language is necessary
   c to show that people prefer other languages

4 Why is English not considered a truly global language by some people?

   a because many people are now proficient in English
   b because many people don't use it for primary communication at home
   c because many people are studying English now

5 What is the speaker's view of English as a global language?

   a that it will continue to be the *lingua franca*, but not replace other languages
   b that it will continue to be the *lingua franca*, and replace other languages
   c that it will not continue to be the *lingua franca* because there are too many varieties

D LISTEN FOR DETAILS Close your book. Watch the lecture again. Add details to your notes and correct any mistakes.

E CHECK YOUR UNDERSTANDING Use your notes. Decide if the statements are T (true) or F (false), based on the lecture. Correct any false statements.

_____ **1** Professor Kachru called the current use of English "unprecedented."

_____ **2** The first point of view presented is that English won't replace other languages.

_____ **3** The other point of view is that, internationally, English is the main language in people's daily lives.

_____ **4** Business schools in France are now fighting hard to keep English out.

_____ **5** More than a billion people speak English as their first language.

_____ **6** India is mentioned as a country where English is an official language.

_____ **7** Most Korean pilots speak English at home instead of Korean.

_____ **8** Currently, 75 countries use English as an official language.

_____ **9** The speaker supports David Crystal's point of view of English as a global language.

_____ **10** The speaker says there must be an international standard for English.

HEAR the language

Stressing Words to Focus the Listener

When we listen, we focus on the stressed words—the most important words. A speaker stresses important words by going up in pitch and saying the words a little more slowly and using slightly increased volume.

> **EXAMPLE**
> *Pilots* in Korea or China may **only** learn the English they **need** on the job.

A LISTEN Listen to the statements and questions from the lecture. Circle the words that the speaker stresses the most. The number of stressed words is in parentheses.

1 (3) It's the common language throughout the world right now as well, isn't it?

2 (4) Professor Braj B. Kachru, an authority on the use of English, called the current global use of English "unprecedented."

3 (4) This means that in the history of the world there has never been one language used by so many people.

4 (7) Supporters of this point of view acknowledge that people all over the world use English every day to communicate in certain domains, like business, or science, or government.

5 (5) Now, in addition, the European Union uses English for both written and spoken communication.

6 (8) Business schools in Europe are now teaching their classes in English—even in France, a country that has fought very hard in the past to keep English out.

7 (7) So, to sum up: We know millions of people throughout the world need a common language to facilitate communication.

8 (6) Now first, according to recent data, more than a billion people speak some English as a second or third language.

9 (4) Even in English-speaking countries, millions of people prefer to speak a language other than English all the time.

10 (4) It's evident that millions of people worldwide know only the English required for specific situations.

B PAIR WORK Work with a partner. Take turns saying the sentences. Pay attention to word stress.

TALK about the topic

Disagreeing

A FOLLOW THE DISCUSSION Watch as the students talk about English as a global language. Read each comment. Then check (✓) the student who makes the comment.

Michael   May   Yhinny   Qiang

	Michael	May	Yhinny	Qiang
1 "You know when the lecturer was talking about languages and culture?"	☐	☐	☐	☐
2 "I need English for class now, or maybe someday at my job."	☐	☐	☐	☐
3 "What about the idea of having an international standard for English?"	☐	☐	☐	☐
4 "It's like a set of rules for grammar, spelling ... that everyone agrees to."	☐	☐	☐	☐

B LEARN THE STRATEGIES Watch the discussion again. Listen closely for the comments. Then check (✓) the discussion strategy the student uses.

	Agreeing	Disagreeing
1 May: "Oh, definitely."	☐	☐
2 Qiang: "Right! I don't see other languages disappearing."	☐	☐
3 May: "Oh, it's the same with me."	☐	☐
4 May: "You're joking, right?"	☐	☐

> **Discussion Strategy**   In most conversations, **expressing disagreement** without seeming to be too disagreeable is key! One way to do so is to first acknowledge the other person's point: *I see what you're saying, but ... .* Or you can be direct: *I simply disagree.* Some people like to soften their position with an apology: *I'm sorry, but ... .* And of course, body language and tone can further "shape" your message.

C TRY IT In a small group, discuss one or more of these topics. Try to use the discussion strategies you have learned.

- Why do you think English has become the common language for globalization?
- Do you agree that as more people learn English, their desire to hold on to their own cultures will get stronger?
- If you were to establish an international standard for English, what would the rules be for grammar? Vocabulary? Pronunciation?

REVIEW your notes

REVIEW *Paraphrase* means to retell something in your own words. With a partner, take turns paraphrasing the main ideas from the lecture. Then use your notes to complete the outline below.

I. Def. of a global language:

II. 1st point of view:

    A. Support:

    B. Support:

    C. Support:

III. Contrasting point of view:

    A. Support:

    B. Support:

    C. Support:

IV. Conclusions:

    A. About the future of English? Other languages?

    B. About the need for an international standard?

TIP!
Remember: Focus on the **similarities** and **differences** between ideas.

Now you are ready to take the Unit Test and the Proficiency Assessment.

EXPRESS your ideas

Varieties of English

There are many varieties of English spoken in the world every day. The main varieties of English are British, North American, West African, East African, South African, Asian-Pacific, South Asian, Australian, and New Zealander English.

TASK **Research one variety of English. Then give a short presentation about your findings. Use examples.**

Prepare

1 Choose a variety of English. (Note that there are varieties other than those listed above. Choose any variety that interests you.) Choose two areas of that variety: the pronunciation, the grammar, the vocabulary, or special expressions, such as idioms. Find an example from the two areas by interviewing someone who speaks the variety. (If you can't find a native speaker, use YouTube or TED Talks or other Internet sources to find examples.) Take notes so you can explain the examples and why you find them interesting.

2 Organize the information from your notes into an outline. (Use the example outline to help you.) Do not write sentences on your outline. Use key words and phrases only.

3 Work with a partner. Compare your outlines. Ask each other questions about the examples. Make changes to your outline as needed.

Practice

4 Practice with a partner. Take turns giving your presentations. Did you follow your outline? Use the *Unit 2 Presentation Evaluation Form* (in Appendix C) to give each other suggestions to improve your presentations.

5 Practice by yourself. Record your presentation or practice in front of a mirror. Use the Evaluation Form to evaluate your presentation.

Present

6 Deliver your presentation to the class. Glance at your outline occasionally and then look at your audience as you speak. Don't read your presentation. Try to speak naturally and confidently.

7 When you finish, ask for audience questions: *Do you have any questions? Is there something you didn't understand?*

8 Listen to your classmates' presentations.

Evaluate

9 Use the Evaluation Form to evaluate your and your classmates' presentations. Be supportive: Give comments that will encourage your classmates to improve!

Presentation Strategy: Using examples

Examples help your audience understand your main ideas by providing clarifying information. An example needs to relate directly to the main idea.

TOPIC: VARIETIES OF ENGLISH

I Introduction
  A Topic
  B Main ideas

II Language difference 1
  A Example
  [*optional:* **B** Explanation]

III Language difference 2
  A Example
  [*optional:* **B** Explanation]

IV Conclusion

3 Phobias

CONNECT to the topic

Are you afraid of anything? Of course you are—we all are! It's natural to be afraid of things we think could harm us. But some fears are very strong and unreasonable. These are called *phobias*. Common phobias include *acrophobia*, a fear of heights, *arachnophobia*, a fear of spiders, and *ophidiophobia*, a fear of snakes.

A THINK ABOUT IT Take this survey about fears and phobias. Check (√) your responses. Then compare responses with a partner. Give reasons.

	Agree	Disagree
• Fear can help us to survive real dangers.	☐	☐
• Our culture teaches us what to be afraid of.	☐	☐
• A fear of fire or a big storm is a normal fear.	☐	☐
• Most people are afraid of trying new things.	☐	☐
• Fear can keep us from achieving our goals.	☐	☐
• If you have a phobia, you should keep it a secret.	☐	☐

B TUNE IN Listen to a conversation between Dan Vasquez, a product engineer, and his boss, Roger Brody. Then work with a partner to answer the questions, based on the conversation.

1 Why does Dan Vasquez want someone from the sales team to make the presentation?

_____

2 What is the main reason Roger Brody wants Vasquez to give the presentation?

_____

3 What does Brody mean by "You're not alone"?

_____

4 What is Brody's advice?

_____

C PAIR WORK Work with a partner. Ask: *What do you think of the boss's advice? Are you afraid of some social situations? What do you do to prepare? What else are you afraid of?*

BUILD your vocabulary

A LISTEN The boldfaced words are from the unit lecture on phobias. Listen to each sentence. Then guess the meaning of the boldfaced word.

1 Mark studied psychology because he was interested in human **behavior**.

2 Shaking is a common **characteristic** of a scared person.

3 Phobias are **classified** into categories including specific fears, such as the fear of dogs, and situational fears, such as the fear of speaking in public.

4 My uncle's fear of public places was **constant**; he never left his house.

5 After seeing an airplane crash, Lydia **developed** aerophobia. She panicked when she even saw an airplane and never flew again.

6 The **duration** of his fear of water was short. After just a few weeks of swimming lessons, he was cured.

7 Jan's **physical** response to the dark was extreme. She would start shaking and sweating as soon as the lights went out.

8 A **psychologist** can help patients with phobias look for deeper problems.

9 Tara couldn't be **rational** when she saw a cat. She couldn't think clearly.

10 When Martin was a boy, he was in a serious car accident. This childhood **trauma** made him too afraid to drive.

B TRY IT Circle the best definition for each boldfaced word.

1 human **behavior**

actions   feelings   ideas

2 two common **characteristics**

features   feelings   problems

3 **classified** into three categories

grouped   dismissed   treated

4 His fear was **constant**.

irregular   continuous   very slow

5 **developed** acrophobia

removed   began to have   recovered from

6 The **duration** was short.

size   *length of time*   *distance*

7 a **physical** response

related to emotions   *related to the body*   *related to feelings*

8 The **psychologist** took care of the patient.

instructor   *sleep researcher*   *person who treats mental problems*

9 too afraid to be **rational**

unreasonable   *reasonable*   *emotional*

10 a childhood **trauma**

interesting experience   *fun experience*   *bad experience*

C PAIR WORK Work with a partner. Read the sentences in Column A and discuss the meanings of the boldfaced phrases. Then read sentences 1–5 aloud as your partner fills in the blanks in Column B. Switch roles for 6–10.

COLUMN A	COLUMN B
1 Phobias are **classified by** the thing that is feared.	**1** Phobias are **classified** _____ the thing that is feared.
2 What's the **definition of** a phobia?	**2** What's the **definition** _____ a phobia?
3 There are various **theories on** the causes of phobias.	**3** There are various **theories** _____ the causes of phobias.
4 An interesting **topic in** psychology is phobias.	**4** An interesting **topic** _____ psychology is phobias.
5 One **type of** phobias is situational phobias.	**5** One **type** _____ phobias is situational phobias.
6 Tomas was injured by a cat and became **afraid of** them.	**6** Tomas was injured by a cat and became **afraid** _____ them.
7 The child's **reaction to** the dark was to cry.	**7** The child's **reaction** _____ the dark was to cry.
8 Some phobias tend to **run in families**.	**8** Some phobias tend to **run** _____ **families**.
9 There are a variety of **treatments for** phobias.	**9** There are a variety of **treatments** _____ phobias.
10 A phobia may be a **sign of** a deep psychological problem.	**10** A phobia may be a **sign** _____ a deep psychological problem.

FOCUS your attention

Key Words

Speakers use a variety of cues to let you know when they are about to focus on a key word in the lecture.

CUES	PHRASES INTRODUCING KEY WORD DEFINITIONS
They may do any of the following:	*One is called ...*
• Pause	*One (example) is ...*
• Slow down	*The first (type) is ...*
• Speak more loudly	
• Repeat the key word	
• Spell the key word	
• Define the key word using an introductory phrase.	

One way to note key words is to write the key word on the left and the definition on the right. Say you hear this: *A phobia—that's p-h-o-b-i-a—is an extreme fear.* Your notes might look like this:

phobia → an extreme fear

🔊 **A TRY IT** Listen to an excerpt from a psychology lecture. Take notes. What key word cues do you hear? What key words?

B PAIR WORK Compare notes and answers with a partner.

WATCH the lecture

Professor Ruth Brooks-Hall

A THINK ABOUT IT You are about to watch the unit lecture on phobias. Why do you think some people develop phobias?

_____

_____

B LISTEN FOR MAIN IDEAS Close your book. Watch the lecture and take notes.

C CHECK YOUR UNDERSTANDING Use your notes. Based on the lecture, which of the statements are true? Make a check mark (√).

☐ **1** A phobia doesn't interfere with someone's life.

☐ **2** Phobias are extreme fears of a common object or situation.

☐ **3** People with phobias often have strong physical reactions.

☐ **4** The speaker discusses two types of phobias: specific and situational.

☐ **5** Psychologists have defined the characteristics of a phobia.

☐ **6** Phobias only run in families.

☐ **7** There's one main reason why all phobias develop.

☐ **8** Psychologists can't successfully treat most phobias.

D LISTEN FOR DETAILS Close your book. Watch the lecture again. Add details to your notes and correct any mistakes.

E CHECK YOUR UNDERSTANDING Use your notes. Choose the word or phrase that best completes each idea, based on the lecture.

1 A phobia is a very strong, very _____ fear.

  a weird
  b focused
  c personal

2 A phobia can often _____ a person's life.

  a help
  b strengthen
  c interfere with

3 A phobia is not a(n) _____ response.

  a necessary
  b rational
  c uncontrollable

4 A phobia will often _____ a long time.

  a last
  b develop over
  c disappear after

5 A person with cynophobia will probably avoid _____ .

  a cats
  b dogs
  c open spaces

6 A boy develops a phobia by watching his father. This is an example of

_____ .

  a direct learning
  b association theory
  c indirect learning

7 A woman fell into a lake when she was a child, and now she won't go near water. This

example shows _____ .

  a indirect learning
  b the association theory
  c that phobias run in families

8 To treat a phobia, a psychologist tries to change the patient's _____ .

  a childhood trauma
  b family situation
  c behavior

HEAR the language

Contractions

In natural speech, speakers may use **contractions** to keep the rhythm of English. Sometimes, it can be difficult to hear or understand.

> **EXAMPLE**
> Today **we are** → **we're**   going to study an interesting topic in psychology: phobias.

A LISTEN Listen to the statements from the lecture. Circle the phrases you hear.

1 A phobia is a fear, yes, but a phobia (**is not / isn't**) a normal fear; it's an extreme fear.

2 She (**could not / couldn't**) ride in an elevator without being terrified.

3 Sometimes (**she would / she'd**) panic and start breathing fast as soon as she got into an elevator.

4 First, a phobia (**is not / isn't**) a rational response.

5 (**She would / She'd**) start sweating and shaking—not a rational response.

6 For example, for Maria, even though when she told herself not to be afraid to ride in the elevator, it (**did not / didn't**) help.

7 (**It is /It's**) an irrational response, (**it is /it's**) long-lasting, and (**it is / it's**) uncontrollable.

8 For example, someone (**could have / could've**) learned to be afraid of dogs if he were attacked and injured by a dog as a child.

9 Well, first, psychologists know that if a (**phobia has been / phobia's been**) learned, it can usually be unlearned.

10 Well, (**that is / that's**) enough for now.

B PAIR WORK Work with a partner. Take turns saying the sentences. Pay attention to the contractions.

TALK about the topic

Keeping a Discussion on Topic

A **FOLLOW THE DISCUSSION** Watch as the students talk about phobias. Read each comment. Then check (√) the student who makes the comment.

Alana   Ayman   Molly   Rob

	Alana	Ayman	Molly	Rob
1 "I don't know if it's a phobia, but I hate spiders. I'm completely terrified of them."	☐	☐	☐	☐
2 "Well, but those are natural reactions, don't you think?"	☐	☐	☐	☐
3 "Un-control-able. So, something that you can't control."	☐	☐	☐	☐
4 "Well, back home we don't believe in getting therapy for these kinds of problems."	☐	☐	☐	☐

B **LEARN THE STRATEGIES** Watch the discussion again. Listen closely for the comments. Then check (√) the discussion strategy the student uses.

	Asking for clarification or confirmation	Keeping a discussion on topic	Offering a fact or example
1 **Ayman:** "Seriously guys ... let's stay focused, OK?"	☐	☐	☐
2 **Rob:** "I'm the same way with snakes ... . I was hiking last summer ... "	☐	☐	☐
3 **Alana:** "Wait ... . What does that mean ... ?"	☐	☐	☐
4 **Ayman:** "That part of the definition made me think of my friend back in Dubai ... . "	☐	☐	☐

Discussion Strategy In study groups or other organized conversations, **keeping a discussion on topic** is in everyone's best interest. While tangents (related topics) can be interesting, it's fair to remind others of the focus. Common expressions include *I'd like to get back to ... , We're getting a little off track ... ,* and the very informal *Anyway!*

C **TRY IT** In a small group, discuss one or more of these topics. Try to use the discussion strategies you have learned.

- Suppose your friend was afraid of revolving doors. What could you do to help?
- Do you know anyone with a phobia? Describe the person's behavior.
- What are some "normal" fears that you, your friends, or family members have?

REVIEW your notes

REVIEW Read your notes. Did you write down the key words and phrases from the lecture? Can you explain them? With a partner, take turns explaining the ideas from the lecture. Then complete the notes below.

- Def. of a phobia:

- Main kinds of phobias:

1)
Ex.:
2)
Ex.:

- Characteristics of a phobia:

1)
2)
3)

- Classification system of phobias:

- Ex.'s of names of phobias:

- 2 theories on causes of phobias:

1)
2)

> **TIP!**
>
> Remember: Words that are louder, repeated, spelled out, or defined are key words—meaning they are key to understanding the main ideas of the lecture.

Now you are ready to take the Unit Test and the Proficiency Assessment.

EXPRESS your ideas

Overcoming a Fear

The professor in the unit lecture talked about phobias. Not everyone has a phobia, but many people have normal fears such as a fear of spiders, snakes, heights, thunderstorms, flying on airplanes, taking exams, and going to the dentist.

TASK Research a common fear and steps for overcoming it. Then give a short presentation, helping your audience "unlearn" the fear by making changes in their behavior. Use sensory details.

Prepare

1 Choose a common fear. Write down a few problems that the fear may cause. Then write down several small steps people can take to overcome this fear. Be creative! Finally, write down several ways your audience members' lives will be better if they take these steps. To convince your audience, be sure to clearly identify the problem and present a step-by-step solution. Remember to use details that will appeal to their senses and emotions.

2 Organize the information from your notes into an outline. (Use the example outline to help you). Do not write sentences on your outline. Use key word and phrases only.

3 Work with a partner. Compare your outlines. Does each supporting detail relate to a main idea?

Practice

4 Practice with a partner. Take turns giving your presentation. Did you follow your outline? Did you use contractions or more formal language? Use the *Unit 3 Presentation Evaluation Form* (in Appendix C) to give each other suggestions to improve your presentations.

5 Practice by yourself. Record your presentation or practice in front of a mirror. Use the Evaluation Form to evaluate your presentation.

Present

6 Deliver your presentation to the class. Glance at your outline occasionally—for example, to remind yourself of the main ideas—and then look at your audience as you speak. Don't read your presentation. Try to speak naturally and confidently.

7 When you finish, ask for audience questions: *Was there anything you didn't follow? Is there anything you need for me to repeat? Are you ready to make these changes?*

8 Listen to your classmates' presentations.

Evaluate

9 Use the Evaluation Form to evaluate your and your classmates' presentations. Be supportive: Give comments that will encourage your classmates to improve!

Presentation Strategy: Describing sensory details

When you want to focus your listeners' attention, you can use sensory details. Sensory details are based on the senses (sight, hearing, smell, taste, feel) and convey, for example, how something smells (*a hint of smoke in the air*) or feels (*the icy cold lake*). These details should be very descriptive. If you are very descriptive, you can appeal to your listeners' senses and emotions.

TOPIC: OVERCOMING A FEAR

I Introduction
  A Topic
  B Main ideas in 1–2 sentences

II Problem: Fear and effect on life
  A 1st problem fear creates for person
  B 2nd problem fear causes
  [*optional:* **C** 3rd problem fear causes]

III Solution
  A Step #1
  B Step #2
  C Step #3
  [*optional:* **D** Step #4]

IV Benefits
  A Benefit #1
  B Benefit #2

V Conclusion: Invitation to audience to make changes

4 Success in the Global Economy

CONNECT to the topic

Have you ever thought about starting a business? What kind of business would you start? Who would your target market be? How would you advertise your business to make it successful?

A THINK ABOUT IT Consider these questions about business. Then compare responses with a partner.

- What kinds of new businesses have you noticed?
- What are some new products and services you use?
- What do you like about them?
- What makes the businesses behind these products and services successful?

B TUNE IN Listen to a radio interview with aspiring entrepreneur Amanda Burns. Then circle the best answer, based on the interview. Compare answers with a partner.

1 Amanda Burns sees a business opportunity in **mobile entertainment / wearable technology / health foods**.

2 Her target market is **grade school children / young teens / adults**.

3 She wants to use a fund-raising website in order to **interest people in her idea / sell her company / find a name for her company**.

4 A good name for her company might be **Feel Fit / Inner Vision / Tru to You**.

C PAIR WORK Work with a partner. Consider the expression "Don't follow a trend, create a trend." Ask: *What does this mean in business? What are some examples of new trends? How did they start?*

BUILD your vocabulary

A LISTEN The boldfaced words are from the unit lecture on success in the global economy. Listen to each sentence. Then choose the meaning of the boldfaced word.

1 Because our company was so successful, a larger company wanted to **acquire** it.

    sell   *buy*   *reduce*

2 A company that can **adapt** quickly to new trends has a better chance of succeeding.

    complete   *reflect*   *change to fit*

3 One **attribute** of a successful business leader is being open to new ideas.

    idea   *quality*   *section*

4 The cause of the sudden price increase was **complex**; there wasn't one simple reason.

    complicated   *simple*   *expensive*

5 **Consumers** like low prices and good quality in the products and services they buy.

    shoppers   *businesspeople*   *citizens*

6 There are a number of **diverse** factors that influence the products people choose to buy.

    lengthy   *considerate*   *very different*

7 Our new business offers both **goods** and services including new and used computers, and computer repairs.

    products   *activities*   *improvements*

8 I'll **illustrate** this characteristic with an example of a successful business in China.

    demonstrate   *perform*   *consume*

9 Business decisions in one country often affect other countries. Their economies are **interrelated**.

    consistent   *connected*   *independent*

10 The stock market was **volatile** last month. One day it went way up; the next day it fell.

    obvious   *unstable*   *reasonable*

B PAIR WORK Work with a partner. Read the sentences in Column A and discuss the meanings of the boldfaced phrases. Then read sentences 1–5 aloud as your partner fills in the blanks in Column B. Switch roles for 6–10.

COLUMN A

1 Education is one **component of** success.

2 What else is needed to be **successful in** today's business environment?

3 This **refers to** a global system.

4 There is **uncertainty about** how people will react.

5 People **tend to** make familiar choices.

6 Companies need to **pay attention to** opportunities.

7 The new phone was successful because it **aligned with** what customers wanted.

8 These are the main **challenges in** business today.

9 How does someone succeed **in the face of** these challenges?

10 What are the **characteristics of** a successful business leader?

COLUMN B

1 Education is one **component** _____ success.

2 What else is needed to be **successful** _____ today's business environment?

3 This **refers** _____ a global system.

4 There is **uncertainty** _____ how people will react.

5 People **tend** _____ make familiar choices.

6 Companies need to **pay attention** _____ opportunities.

7 The new phone was successful because it **aligned** _____ what customers wanted.

8 These are the main **challenges** _____ business today.

9 How does someone succeed **in the face** _____ these challenges?

10 What are the **characteristics** _____ a successful business leader?

FOCUS your attention

Topics and Subtopics

In a lecture, there is usually one main topic and one or more subtopics. Subtopics are divisions or aspects of the main topic. For example, if the main topic is *success in business*, two subtopics might be *leadership skills* and *team building*. At the beginning of a lecture, a speaker often describes how the subtopics will be presented. Listen carefully to understand how the lecture will be organized.

INTRODUCING TOPICS AND SUBTOPICS

Today we're going to talk about *success in business.* (main topic) ***I want to focus first on*** *the leadership skills needed to succeed.* (subtopic) ***Then I plan to consider*** *ways to build a strong team of loyal employees.* (subtopic)

This afternoon I'm going to discuss *success in business.* (main topic) ***Specifically, we'll look at two aspects:*** *how to build a customer base* (subtopic) *and ways to attract investors.* (subtopic)

One way to take notes is to write the topic, and then indent the subtopics below. For example:

(topic) *success in business*
    (subtopic) *leadership skills*
    (subtopic) *team building*

A TRY IT Listen to an excerpt from a talk about success in business. Take notes. What is the main topic? What are the subtopics?

B PAIR WORK Compare notes with a partner. Use your notes to answer the questions.

WATCH the lecture

Professor Nancy Lee

A THINK ABOUT IT You are about to watch the unit lecture on success in the global economy. What characteristics are most important for a person to have in order to succeed in business?

_____

_____

B LISTEN FOR MAIN IDEAS Close your book. Watch the lecture and take notes.

C CHECK YOUR UNDERSTANDING Use your notes. Answer the questions, based on the lecture. Circle *a*, *b*, or *c*.

1 In what order did the speaker talk about these ideas?

  a characteristics of successful leaders, characteristics of the global economy, examples of successful businesses

  b examples of successful businesses, characteristics of the global economy, characteristics of successful leaders

  c characteristics of the global economy, characteristics of successful leaders, examples of successful businesses

2 What does the speaker mean by a VUCA environment? Circle TWO answers.

  a a setting in which education is necessary for success
  b a situation in which economic conditions change rapidly
  c an atmosphere in which the economic factors are interrelated

3 What is the main reason the speaker describes VUCA Prime?

  a to explain why there is volatility
  b to show how uncertain the economy is
  c to explain the qualities needed for success

4 What is the speaker referring to when she says "what else is needed" to be successful?

  a education
  b money
  c characteristics

5 What is the speaker's opinion of the business leaders mentioned?

  a They don't have all the information they need.
  b They tend to make familiar choices.
  c They understand how to succeed in today's economy.

Jeff Bezos, founder of Amazon.com

D **LISTEN FOR DETAILS** Close your book. Watch the lecture again. Add details to your notes and correct any mistakes.

E **CHECK YOUR UNDERSTANDING** Use your notes. Decide if the statements are *T* (*true*) or *F* (*false*), based on the lecture. Correct any false statements.

_____ **1** The speaker believes several factors contribute to someone's business success.

_____ **2** Ambiguity means the economy is likely to change suddenly.

_____ **3** Another way to say "today's economy" is "the global economy."

_____ **4** Consumers' mixed reaction to Google Glass is an example of uncertainty.

_____ **5** Walmart didn't succeed in Germany because its prices were too high.

_____ **6** The "ambiguity effect" means people prefer to choose familiar things.

_____ **7** Seeing the rapid growth of the Internet gave Jeff Bezos the vision to start Amazon.

_____ **8** The founder of SlideShare wanted people to be able to shop online more easily.

_____ **9** Laura Fitton understood the importance of using social media for marketing.

_____ **10** Pierre Omidyar's ability to quickly adapt his Ebay website showed agility.

HEAR the language

Reduced Vowels

In English, unstressed vowels are often **reduced** to the neutral schwa sound /ə/, like you hear in the first syllable of *continue* [kən tɪn yu]. Reducing unstressed vowels is a natural part of fluent English pronunciation.

> **EXAMPLE**
> *Today we're going to talk about how to succeed in today's economy.*

A LISTEN Listen to the statements and questions from the lecture. Circle the reduced /ə/ sounds you hear in the underlined words. The number of sounds is in parentheses.

1 (3) Of course, we all know that <u>education</u> is only one <u>component</u> of success.

2 (3) First, I want to survey the <u>current</u> <u>business</u> <u>environment</u>.

3 (2) When we talk about "<u>today's</u> <u>economy</u>," what do we mean?

4 (3) Well, basically we're <u>referring</u> to a <u>global</u> <u>system</u> of people, resources, and ideas.

5 (3) They <u>believed</u> that <u>consumers</u> would love it.

6 (2) <u>Around</u> that same time, the public was getting nervous about <u>privacy</u>.

7 (4) For example, a <u>company</u> may have a <u>problem</u> in a foreign country because of <u>customs</u> or <u>cultural</u> values the company did not understand.

8 (4) People tend to make <u>familiar</u> choices because they don't like <u>ambiguity</u>.

9 (3) <u>Vision</u> means making big <u>decisions</u> that <u>align</u> with this dream.

10 (2) Which VUCA Prime <u>qualities</u> do you <u>possess</u>?

B PAIR WORK Work with a partner. Take turns saying the sentences. Pay attention to the reduced vowels.

TALK about the topic

Trying to Reach a Consensus

A FOLLOW THE DISCUSSION Watch as the students talk about business success. Read each opinion. Then check (✓) who expresses it.

Shelley   Ben   Kenzie   Hugh

	Shelley	Ben	Kenzie	Hugh
1 Envisioning a clear direction of the company is most important.	☐	☐	☐	☐
2 You have to be able to think quickly and respond to what people want.	☐	☐	☐	☐
3 Paying attention to how things are connected is vital for success.	☐	☐	☐	☐

B LEARN THE STRATEGIES Watch the discussion again. Listen closely for the comments. Then check (✓) the discussion strategy the student uses.

	Asking for clarification or confirmation	Paraphrasing	Trying to reach a consensus
1 Shelley: "Can anyone explain what the professor meant by a VUCA environment?"	☐	☐	☐
2 Ben: "In short, VUCA means a challenging, rapidly changing business environment."	☐	☐	☐
3 Hugh: "When the professor said 'today's economy,' what does that mean?"	☐	☐	☐
4 Kenzie: "I think it means the current business environment."	☐	☐	☐
5 Shelley: "So it sounds like we don't agree about order ... . But I'm sure we *do* agree that all four VUCA Prime qualities are necessary in a good business leader. Don't we?"	☐	☐	☐

Discussion Strategy Getting a group to **reach a consensus**, or agree, can be challenging. One approach is to use questions to identify areas of agreement (*So, when is everyone free to meet again?*). You can follow up by making suggestions based on feedback (*Sounds like Sunday is open for everyone—does that work?*).

C TRY IT In a small group, discuss one or more of these topics. Try to use the discussion strategies you have learned.

- What do you see as the biggest challenges in starting a business?
- What are the most effective ways to use social media in launching a business?
- What are the advantages and disadvantages of working at a small start-up company versus at a large, established business?

REVIEW your notes

REVIEW Work with a partner. Use your notes to complete this outline of the lecture. Include information on topics and subtopics. Then work together to retell the main ideas.

I. Success in today's economy:

   1) the current business environment

   2) the attributes needed in order to be successful

II. VUCA—factors to consider:

   1) Volatility: _____

   2) Uncertainty: _____

   3) Complexity: _____

   4) Ambiguity: _____

III. VUCA Prime—characteristics:

   1) Vision: _____

   2) Understanding: _____

   3) Clarity: _____

   4) Agility: _____

IV. Examples of successful leaders

   1) _____

   2) _____

   3) _____

   4) _____

V. Conclusion about what is needed to succeed in business

TIP!
Subtopics are aspects of the main topic. Review details of each subtopic to help you understand the focus of the lecture.

Now you are ready to take the Unit Test and the Proficiency Assessment.

EXPRESS your ideas

Formula for Success

In this unit, you learned about characteristics needed for success in our global economy. What characteristics do you think are most important for being successful in business?

TASK Brainstorm a business you would like to start. Then give a short presentation about it. Preview the structure of your presentation with your introduction.

Prepare

1 Think of a business you would like to start and the product or service your business will offer. Describe it. Decide on your target market. Then think about how to convince your audience that your business will be successful. Decide which characteristics of VUCA Prime you possess and how you can use these to persuade your audience to invest.

2 Organize the information from your brainstorm into an outline. (Use the example outline to help you). Do not write sentences on your outline. Use key words and phrases only.

3 Work with a partner. Talk about your business and your plan for success by comparing your outlines and discussing your key ideas. Make changes to your outline as needed.

Practice

4 Practice with a partner. Take turns giving your presentations. Did you follow your outline? Did you state your main ideas clearly in your introduction? Use the *Unit 4 Presentation Evaluation Form* (in Appendix C) to give each other suggestions to improve your presentations.

5 Practice by yourself. Record your presentation or practice in front of a mirror. Use the Evaluation Form to evaluate your presentation.

Present

6 Deliver your presentation to the class. Glance at your outline occasionally and then look at your audience as you speak. Don't read your presentation. Try to speak naturally and confidently.

7 When you finish, ask for audience questions: *Are there any questions? Would you like me to clarify anything?*

8 Listen to your classmates' presentations.

Evaluate

9 Use the Evaluation Form to evaluate your and your classmates' presentations. Be supportive: Give comments that will encourage your classmates to improve!

Presentation Strategy: Developing an introduction

A good introduction tells your listeners the structure of your presentation. In your introduction, clearly state the main ideas you plan to discuss. Don't give any supporting details in your introduction. Remember, your listeners don't have your presentation outline. They need you to signal your most important ideas and the order you plan to discuss them. Here are some phrases you might use to introduce your main ideas:

Today, I'm going to discuss a, b, and c.

My presentation is going to focus on a, b, and c.

This afternoon, we're going to talk about a, b, and c.

TOPIC: FORMULA FOR SUCCESS

I Introduction: Main ideas

II Vision
  A Description of product or service
    1 Detail
    2 Detail
  B Development of product or service
    1 Detail
    2 Detail

III Understanding
  A Current market
    1 Detail
    2 Detail
    [*optional:* **3** Detail]
  B Opportunities
    1 Detail
    2 Detail
    [*optional:* **3** Detail]

IV Clarity
  A Most important step
    1 Detail
    2 Detail
    [*optional:* **3** Detail]
  B Next important step
    1 Detail
    2 Detail
    [*optional:* **3** Detail]

V Conclusion: Review of main ideas

5 How We Each Learn Best

CONNECT to the topic

We sometimes hear "Oh, she's really intelligent" or "He's so intelligent." But what do the terms "intelligent" and "intelligence" actually mean? Is it something that can be determined by a test? Many people believe that there are different *kinds* of intelligence.

A THINK ABOUT IT Read these statements about learning. Score them:
3 = This describes me. 2 = This is me sometimes. 1 = This isn't me at all.
Then compare responses with a partner. Do your scores reflect how you learn best?

Statement	Score
• I don't read instructions—I like to figure out how things work.	
• I like working alone better than in a group.	
• I enjoy creating things.	
• I love to dance and listen to music.	
• I'm good at understanding other people's feelings.	
• I'd rather spend time exploring nature than reading about it.	
• I have a good sense of direction.	
• I can use charts and graphs to understand information quickly.	

B TUNE IN Listen to a conversation between two friends, Sasha and Hector. Then answer the questions, based on the conversation. Compare answers with a partner.

1 Why is the room a mess?

_____

2 What does Hector mean by "I learn by doing"?

_____

3 How are Sasha's and Hector's approaches different?

_____

C PAIR WORK Work with a partner. Ask: *Who are you more like: Sasha or Hector? Think about these abilities: dancing, athletics, languages, understanding other people, solving math problems, music. Which are you good at? Are some abilities more valued than others? Which ones and why?*

LEARNING OUTCOMES
In this unit you will:
- identify numbered lists in a short talk
- note main ideas from an education lecture
- extract details from an education lecture
- identify and practice final -*s* and -*ed* sounds
- recognize and practice strategies for expressing your opinion
- review with a partner to prepare for the unit test
- give a presentation about your learning style, using transitions

BUILD your vocabulary

A LISTEN The boldfaced words are from the unit lecture on multiple intelligences. Listen to each sentence. Then guess the meaning of the boldfaced word. Work with a partner.

1 Some people don't think traditional IQ tests **accurately** determine intelligence. They believe other kinds of measurement are necessary.

2 To **assess** Darla's speaking ability, the teacher asked her to give an interpretation of a poem. After Darla finished, the teacher gave her a high score.

3 Ken is very **aware** of his own emotions and needs. He knows, for example, that being in a large room full of strangers makes him uncomfortable.

4 The new student has strong verbal intelligence. He **demonstrated** this by writing an excellent report and then presenting it to the class.

5 I have strong **kinesthetic** intelligence. I prefer "hands-on" learning—that is, learning by moving and doing.

6 Using **logic** is one sign of mathematical intelligence. While many people can work with numbers, not everyone can use reason.

7 My cousin can look at a map briefly and get a **mental** image of how the trails all connect.

8 Some educators reject the **notion** that standardized tests are unfair. They believe that this idea is simply wrong.

9 Ms. Kline gave the students two **options** to choose from: They could write a summary of the lecture, or they could make a chart of the key points.

10 Most schools **value** the ability to speak and write well more than they care about artistic or musical ability.

B **TRY IT** Match each phrase with the correct meaning.

_____ **1 accurately** determine   **a** offer a choice in a situation

_____ **2 assess** a student's ability   **b** make a judgment; test

_____ **3** be **aware** of   **c** consider (the ability) important

_____ **4 demonstrate** intelligence   **d** learning by moving

_____ **5 kinesthetic** learning   **e** correctly measure

_____ **6** use **logic**   **f** a picture in the mind

_____ **7 mental** image   **g** not accept an idea

_____ **8** reject a **notion**   **h** use sensible reasons

_____ **9** give an **option**   **i** show ability or skill

_____ **10 value** the ability   **j** realize something exists or is true

C **PAIR WORK** Take turns saying the sentences with a partner. Notice the boldfaced words. Choose the best word to complete each sentence.

1 First we'll be (**go** / **going**) **over** the theory of multiple intelligences.

2 The theory has had a major **impact** (**on** / **for**) teachers.

3 Keep (**at** / **in**) **mind** that some psychologists don't agree with the theory.

4 IQ (**stands** / **stood**) **for** "intelligence quotient."

5 No one in my family is **good** (**at** / **on**) taking tests.

6 We can **think** (**of** / **for**) _inter_personal as meaning between people and _intra_personal as meaning within one person.

7 A high IQ test score is typically **interpreted to** (**mean** / **be**) that the person is intelligent.

8 Doing a (**various** / **variety**) **of** activities instead of just one kind is a good teaching practice.

9 Some people are (**sense** / **sensitive**) **to** the colors around them.

10 This (**brings** / **bring**) **up** other issues, such as standardized tests.

FOCUS your attention

Numbered Lists

A speaker often tells you how many ideas will be covered in a lecture. This provides you with a framework to use as you listen. For example, if the speaker tells you, *I'm going to present four factors*, you know how many factors to listen for and take notes on.

> **NUMBERED LIST SIGNALS**
>
> *There are **five steps** in the process ...*
>
> *I'm going to present **two techniques** ...*
>
> *I'm going to cover **three types** of learning styles ...*

One way to organize your notes is to write down the numbers and key phrases indicated by the speaker. Leave space in between to add short descriptions and details as you listen to the lecture. Writing down a number makes it easier to keep track of the main ideas and remember them later. Say you hear, *I'm going to present two types of learning: auditory learning—learning by listening—and kinesthetic learning—learning by doing.* Your notes might look like this:

---

2 Types of learning

1 Auditory learning (by listening)

2 Kinesthetic learning (by doing)

A TRY IT Listen to an excerpt from a lecture on teaching techniques. What numbers and phrases do you hear? Take notes.

B PAIR WORK How did you organize your notes? Compare notes with a partner.

WATCH the lecture

Professor Nadine Clarke

A THINK ABOUT IT You are about to watch the unit lecture on multiple intelligences. What do you think the term *multiple intelligences* means?

_____

_____

B LISTEN FOR MAIN IDEAS Close your book. Watch the lecture and take notes.

C CHECK YOUR UNDERSTANDING Use your notes. Decide if the statements are *T* (true) or *F* (false), based on the lecture. Correct any false statements.

____ **1** Psychologists know IQ tests are the best way to accurately measure intelligence.

____ **2** Dr. Gardner and others think of "an intelligence" as a strength a person has.

____ **3** People are all different. We all have different intelligences.

____ **4** A good teacher emphasizes verbal and mathematical intelligences because they are the most important.

____ **5** Teachers who accept the theory of multiple intelligences use a variety of teaching techniques.

____ **6** A written test is the best way for students to show that they understand a lesson.

D LISTEN FOR DETAILS Close your book. Watch the lecture again. Add details to your notes and correct any mistakes.

E CHECK YOUR UNDERSTANDING Use your notes. Choose the word or phrase that best completes each idea, based on the lecture.

1 Having "intelligence" means _____ .

    having a good education   *being smart*   *having a strong ability in an area*

2 A score of _____ on an intelligence test is average.

    130   100   113

3 One factor that can affect someone's IQ test score is _____ .

    musical ability   *cultural background*   *height*

4 Someone who uses logic to solve problems has strong _____ intelligence.

    artistic   *verbal*   *mathematical*

5 When Ken watches movies, he pays more attention to the soundtrack than to what

the actors say. He seems to have stronger _____ intelligence than

_____ intelligence.

musical / verbal　　　　　　*verbal / musical*　　　　　　*kinesthetic / verbal*

6 Someone with strong spatial intelligence would be good at _____ .

learning a new language　　　　*reading a map*　　　　*doing something hands-on*

7 Daniel is a good group leader. He works well with his classmates. He has strong

_____ intelligence.

kinesthetic　　　　　　*interpersonal*　　　　　　*intrapersonal*

8 Intrapersonal intelligence is directed toward _____ .

the group　　　　　　*the classroom*　　　　　　*oneself*

9 When Mrs. Sanchez has her students go outside and walk around, she is having them use

_____ intelligence.

artistic　　　　　　*kinesthetic*　　　　　　*spatial*

10 To assess her students, Mrs. Sanchez lets them choose any option they want as long as it is

_____ .

written clearly　　　　　　*drawn well*　　　　　　*about what she taught*

HEAR the language

Final -s and -ed Sounds

The pronunciation of the **final -s** varies depending on the sound that comes immediately before the -s. For example, the -s may sound like /z/ as in *stays*, like /s/ as in *plants*, or like /əz/ as in *kisses*.

Similarly, the pronunciation of the **final -ed** varies depending on the sound that comes immediately before the -ed. For example, the -ed may sound like /d/ as in *stayed*, like /t/ as in *kissed*, or like /əd/ as in *planted*.

EXAMPLES		
flowers /z/	*oranges* /əz/	*stayed* /d/
books /s/	*planted* /əd/	*kissed* /t/

A LISTEN Listen to the statements and questions from the lecture. Circle the sound you hear at the end of each boldfaced word.

1 It's the theory of multiple **intelligences**.

/s/ /z/ /əz/

2 Then, I plan to present how the theory has affected what some **teachers** now do in the classroom.

/s/ /z/ /əz/

3 IQ, by the way, **stands** for "intelligence quotient."

/s/ /z/ /əz/

4 A high score on an IQ test, say 130, is **interpreted** to mean a person is very intelligent.

/d/ /t/ /əd/

5 Harvard University's Dr. Howard Gardner and others have **explored** the notion that we each have many types of intelligence.

/d/ /t/ /əd/

6 People with strong artistic intelligence are sensitive to color, light, and **shapes**.

/s/ /z/ /əz/

7 It's **related** to moving, to learning and remembering information by doing.

/d/ /t/ /əd/

8 What **works** best for one student might not work best for another.

/s/ /z/ /əz/

9 Finally, she teaches them a song about **trees**.

/s/ /z/ /əz/

10 Did you get which intelligences she **worked** with when they went outside?

/d/ /t/ /əd/

B PAIR WORK Work with a partner. Take turns saying the sentences. Pay attention to the final -s and final -ed endings.

TALK about the topic

Expressing an Opinion

A **FOLLOW THE DISCUSSION** Watch as the students talk about intelligence. Read each opinion. Then check (✓) who agrees with it. More than one student may agree.

Qiang   Yhinny   Michael   May

	Qiang	Yhinny	Michael	May
1 A sculptor has talent, not intelligence.	☐	☐	☐	☐
2 Having a high IQ doesn't mean you're good at doing something.	☐	☐	☐	☐
3 The multiple intelligences theory is more useful than an IQ test.	☐	☐	☐	☐

B **LEARN THE STRATEGIES** Watch the discussion again. Listen closely for the comments. Then check (✓) the discussion strategy the student uses.

	Asking for clarification or confirmation	Expressing an opinion	Offering a fact or example
1 May: "What do you mean?"	☐	☐	☐
2 Yhinny: "Can you give me an example?"	☐	☐	☐
3 Michael: "OK. So, for example, this guy Anthony in my history class … "	☐	☐	☐
4 Qiang: "But, he's intelligent in some other way, you think?"	☐	☐	☐
5 May: "I don't think education is for developing those talents. … I'm sorry, that's just how I see it."	☐	☐	☐

Discussion Strategy   In an academic setting, you have numerous opportunities to **express your opinions**—your thoughts, feelings, and positions. But while many opinions start with expressions like *I think, I believe,* and *In my opinion,* it's important to continue with facts, experiences, and other forms of support! This is especially important if you disagree with what someone else has said.

C **TRY IT** In a small group, discuss one or more of these topics. Try to use the discussion strategies you have learned.

- Think about how you learn. Which intelligences are strong for you?
- Teachers guide students to help them learn. When you were younger, was there something that was difficult for you to learn? What would have made it easier for you?
- Should scores on standardized tests be used for entrance to universities?

REVIEW your notes

REVIEW How did you write down the important information? With a partner, take turns explaining the ideas from the lecture as you complete these notes.

Def. of multiple intelligences:

Traditional way to measure intelligence:

Reasons some people don't like:

9 intelligences:

1)   6)

2)   7)

3)   8)

4)   9)

5)

2 effects of multiple intelligences theory in classroom:
1)

2)

Issue with standardized tests:

> **TIP!**
> Numbers help provide a framework of the lecture. Your notes should contain key information for each numbered intelligence mentioned.

Now you are ready to take the Unit Test and the Proficiency Assessment.

EXPRESS your ideas

My Learning Strengths

The lecturer for this unit spoke about nine intelligences—or learning strengths. She explained that we each have all nine, but typically one or more are stronger. How do you use your strengths to accomplish tasks or learn something new?

TASK Consider your learning strengths. Then give a short presentation about how you use your learning strengths to accomplish or learn something. Use transitions.

Prepare

1 Use your notes to review the nine intelligences. Then complete the questionnaire on page 133. This will help you to determine your strengths.

2 Think of something you have accomplished or feel proud of learning. How did you do it? Which strengths did you use?

3 Organize your outline. Include the skill or activity, and how your learning strengths played a role in your accomplishment. Include transition words or phrases to introduce your main ideas and examples.

4 Work with a partner. Compare your outlines. Talk about each other's accomplishments and the learning strengths you used. Ask each other questions. Make changes to your outline as needed.

Practice

5 Practice with your partner. Take turns. Pay attention to whether your partner uses clear transition signals to introduce the accomplishment and each learning strength. Use the *Unit 5 Presentation Evaluation Form* (in Appendix C) to give each other suggestions to improve your presentations.

6 Practice by yourself. Pay attention to the transition signals you use. Did you use a variety of transition words and phrases? Use the Evaluation Form to evaluate your presentation.

Present

7 Deliver your presentation to the class. Use your outline. Occasionally look at your outline to recall the transition words and phrases you chose. Don't read your presentation. Try to speak confidently.

8 Ask for audience questions. When you finish, ask: *Was everything clear? Do you have any ideas for other ways I can use my learning strengths?*

Evaluate

9 Use the Evaluation Form to evaluate your and your classmates' presentations. Be supportive: Give comments that will encourage your classmates to improve!

Presentation Strategy: Moving from one point to the next

Using transition words or phrases is important because they signal your audience that you are concluding one idea and beginning another idea.

First of all, ...

My next learning strength is ...

Next let's discuss (talk about), ...

Finally, ...

TOPIC: MY LEARNING STRENGTHS

Introduction: Description of what I accomplished or learned

Transition to first learning strength
 I First learning strength
   A Learning strength I needed to use
   B How my learning strength helped me succeed

Transition to second learning strength
 II Second learning strength
   A Learning strength I needed to use
   B How my learning strength helped me succeed

[*optional:* Transition to third learning strength]
 III Third learning strength
   A Learning strength I needed to use
   B How my learning strength helped me succeed]

Transition to conclusion
 IV Summary of what I learned and my learning strengths

6

The Silk Road

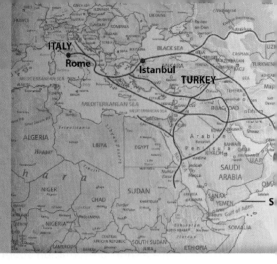

CONNECT to the topic

The Silk Road was a major trade route between China and Europe through Central Asia. This network of roads went through vast deserts and steep mountain ranges. Traders were always searching for the fastest and safest routes. Imagine how difficult it was to travel through this desolate terrain.

A THINK ABOUT IT Look at the map of the Silk Road, above. With a partner, follow the routes from Xi'an, formerly known as Chang'an, to Istanbul and Rome. What geographical features might make these routes challenging? Pay attention to the geographical features as you locate these places:

- regions: Europe, Asia
- countries: India, Italy, China, Turkey
- cities: Xi'an, Dunhuang, Kashgar, Rome, Istanbul
- deserts: the Gobi Desert, the Taklamakan Desert
- mountains: the Pamir Mountains

B TUNE IN Listen to a podcast interview with Todd Warren, who just returned from a bicycle trip. Then work with a partner to answer the questions, based on the interview.

1 Todd Warren has just returned from a bicycle trip in **Europe / China / Turkey**.

2 He rode his bicycle for **two days / two weeks / two months**.

3 He discovered that the Silk Road is **one long road / a network of routes / still full of traders**.

4 He thinks that **China / the Internet / global travel** is a new kind of Silk Road.

C PAIR WORK Work with a partner. Ask: *Would you be interested in traveling on the Silk Road? What other historic travel tours would you like to take during your life?*

LEARNING OUTCOMES
In this unit you will:

■ extract dates and numbers from a short talk

■ recognize main ideas from a history lecture

■ fact-check statements from a history lecture

■ identify and practice using thought groups

■ recognize and practice strategies for paraphrasing

■ review and summarize your lecture notes to prepare for the unit test

■ give a presentation about an important historical figure, using a timeline and a strong conclusion

BUILD your vocabulary

A LISTEN The boldfaced words are from the unit lecture on the Silk Road. Listen to each sentence. Then guess the meaning of the boldfaced word.

1 The Silk Road was a large **network** of interconnected routes. People could travel between China and Rome through various roads that came together.

2 Some traders stayed on the northern route of the Silk Road. Others took an **alternate** route to the south. Both routes led to the Mediterranean Sea.

3 The Han **Dynasty** controlled China for nearly 400 years. Under this powerful family's control, China developed trade with Europe.

4 During the Han Dynasty, the Chinese army was engaged in a **conflict** with Mongol invaders from the north. They fought for many years.

5 The army needed to **recruit** more fighters so that it would have enough soldiers to defend northern China.

6 In 138 BCE, Emperor Wudi sent a group to western China, where the group's leader was held prisoner for a **decade**. The emperor was surprised when the leader returned after those ten years.

7 As the Silk Road developed, the Romans and the Chinese were pushing east and west, **respectively**. In other words, the Romans went east toward China, while the Chinese went west toward Rome.

8 The years of the Tang Dynasty were the **peak** period for the Silk Road. It was most heavily used during that time.

9 The Chinese city of Chang'an (now called Xi'an) was very **prosperous**. Lots of money and goods flowed into Chang'an from many countries.

10 Around 900 CE, trade along the Silk Road started to **decline** sharply. Trade decreased because ongoing fighting made it unsafe to travel.

TRY IT Complete each sentence with the correct word.

decade	decline	network	prosperous	recruit

1 The government needed to _____ more men for the army.

2 Traders traveled various directions through a _____ of routes.

3 Many people became _____ and could buy luxury goods.

4 Trade increased for hundreds of years, but then started to _____ .

5 Instead of saying "the years 1990 to 1999," people often refer to that

_____ as "the 90s."

alternate	conflict	dynasties	peak	respectively

6 A _____ between two countries can last for many years.

7 China was ruled by different _____ for thousands of years.

8 There were many traders in Rome and Chang'an—in other words, from Italy and China,

_____ .

9 During _____ travel on the Silk Road, large caravans of camels with

traders left Chang'an daily.

10 A bad sandstorm developed in the desert, and so the traders took a(n)

_____ route.

C **PAIR WORK** Read the sentences with a partner. Notice the boldfaced words. Then choose a pair of particles to complete each sentence.

from / in	to / in	in / for	of / of

1 The Han Dynasty was _____ **power** _____ several

hundred **years**.

2 The routes **led** _____ trade centers _____ **Europe**.

3 There are different **estimates** _____ the total **length**

_____ the Silk Road.

4 Romans wanted luxury goods _____ **China**, silk _____

particular.

through / in	both / and	against / from

5 It was difficult to **defend** China _____ the Mongol invaders

_____ **the north**.

6 The traders **passed** _____ many small towns _____

Central Asia.

7 The traders exchanged _____ goods _____ trade secrets.

FOCUS your attention

Dates and Numbers

Many history lectures include dates, numbers, and chronologies—or series of events. In a lecture like this, it is important to keep track of the key idea or information associated with each date or number you hear.

CE stands for "Common Era." It is a relatively new term that is being used more and more, and it is expected to eventually replace *AD*. *AD* is an abbreviation for the Latin phrase *Anno Domini*, which means "the year of the Lord" in English. CE and AD have the same meaning. 2017 CE = 2017 AD. BCE stands for "Before the Common Era." It is expected to eventually replace *BC*, which means "Before Christ." *BC* and *BCE* also have the same meaning.

EXAMPLES OF HOW THESE TERMS MIGHT SOUND:

206 BCE = Two-oh-six b-c-e

1368 CE = thirteen-sixty-eight c-e

One way to organize your notes is to write dates, key phrases, and details in separate columns. Leave space to add to your notes as you listen to the lecture. For example:

China

Dates	Key phrase	Details
206 BCE–220 CE	Han Dynasty	Silk Road developed
618–907 CE	Tang Dynasty	peak period of the Silk Road
1368 CE	Ming Dynasty	in power; trade drops off

A TRY IT Listen to an excerpt from a history lecture. What dates and events do you hear? What details? Take notes.

B PAIR WORK Compare notes with a partner. Answer the questions.

WATCH the lecture

Professor Martin Sera

A **THINK ABOUT IT** You are about to watch the unit lecture on the Silk Road. During the time of the Silk Road, no one called it "the Silk Road." The name was given by German geographer Ferdinand von Richthofen in the 19th century. Why do you think he chose the name "the Silk Road"?

_____

_____

B **LISTEN FOR MAIN IDEAS** Close your book. Watch the lecture and take notes.

C **CHECK YOUR UNDERSTANDING** Use your notes. Answer the questions, based on the lecture. Circle *a*, *b*, or *c*.

1 What is the main topic of the lecture?

  a why Chinese goods were popular
  b how the Silk Road developed
  c where the Silk Road was located

2 What was the main reason the Han government wanted to head west initially?

  a to sell gold
  b to get horses
  c to sell spices

3 Who conducted most of the trade?

  a traders from China
  b traders from Rome
  c traders from Central Asia

4 What two things did traders try to avoid?

  a bad people, bad weather
  b bad weather, bad roads
  c bad roads, low-quality goods

5 What were the two main reasons trade on the Silk Road stopped?

  a Silk was no longer popular, and luxury goods were too expensive.
  b The weather was too dangerous, and there were too many robberies.
  c There was too much fighting, and traders started to prefer ships.

D **LISTEN FOR DETAILS** Close your book. Watch the lecture again. Add details to your notes and correct any mistakes.

Istanbul, once at the west end of the Silk Road, is still a major crossroads for trade and culture today.

E **CHECK YOUR UNDERSTANDING** Use your notes. Decide if the statements are
T (true) or *F* (false), based on the lecture. Correct any false statements.

_____ **1** The Silk Road was a major trade route for about 1,000 years.

_____ **2** Trade between Europe and China increased significantly in 200 BCE.

_____ **3** Both Rome and Istanbul are mentioned as important trade centers.

_____ **4** The speaker gave an estimated distance of 5,000 miles (8,000 kilometers) for the Silk Road.

_____ **5** In 138 BCE, Emperor Wudi of the Han Dynasty sent a group to western China to expand trade.

_____ **6** Traders wanted to avoid the Taklamakan Desert.

_____ **7** Most of the traders went short distances.

_____ **8** At the Silk Road's peak popularity, about 2 million people lived in Chang'an, including 6,000 foreigners.

_____ **9** By the 600s, the Tang Dynasty had lost control.

_____ **10** Trade on the Silk Road stopped by 1368.

HEAR the language

Thought Groups

A speaker pauses briefly between **thought groups**. This helps you to understand the ideas as you listen.

> **EXAMPLE**
> *The Silk Road was a major trade route / between Europe and western China / for about 1,500 years /*

A LISTEN Listen to the statements from the lecture. Use a slash (/) to mark the speaker's pauses in each sentence. Note that punctuation indicating a pause has been removed.

1 (4) First I want to mention three dynasties in China that were in power at significant points in the Silk Road's history

2 (4) So from Chang'an the route went west until traders reached the Taklamakan Desert

3 (5) To avoid it some routes went south through Dunhuang and some went north through the Gobi Desert and over into Central Asia

4 (5) The routes all reconnected further west though and eventually they led to some big trade centers in Europe in Rome and what is now called Istanbul in Turkey

5 (4) And when he returned a decade later he told the emperor about a type of big strong horse in western China

6 (6) So you see in about 100 BCE the Romans and the Chinese were pushing east and west respectively and thus the Silk Road developed

7 (5) For example there were trade secrets like where to get the best silk and where the best routes were

8 (5) The Silk Road was very difficult to travel and traders tried alternative routes mainly to avoid two things bad weather and bad people

9 (4) By the early 900s the Tang Dynasty lost power and trade on the Silk Road declined sharply because there was fighting and it became much too dangerous for the traders

10 (4) So to wrap up The Silk Road developed because people in one part of the world wanted something from another part of the world

B PAIR WORK Work with a partner. Take turns saying the sentences. Pay attention to thought groups.

TALK about the topic

Paraphrasing

A FOLLOW THE DISCUSSION Watch as the students talk about the Silk Road. Read each comment. Then check (✓) the student who makes the comment.

Ayman   Molly   Rob   Alana

	Ayman	Molly	Rob	Alana
1 "I'd heard of the Silk Road before, but I had no idea it was so complicated!"	☐	☐	☐	☐
2 "So it was in use for about 1,500 years, and it was about 5,000 miles long altogether."	☐	☐	☐	☐
3 "It was probably a pretty dangerous job, too, I mean, if you think about it ... "	☐	☐	☐	☐

B LEARN THE STRATEGIES Watch the discussion again. Listen closely for the comments. Then check (✓) the discussion strategy the student uses. More than one answer may be correct.

	Asking for opinions or ideas	Offering a fact or example	Paraphrasing
1 **Alana:** "I think I got the general idea—that China wanted goods from Europe, and Europe wanted goods from China, and therefore the Silk Road was developed."	☐	☐	☐
2 **Alana:** "So, do you guys think the Silk Road is famous because of the goods traded?"	☐	☐	☐
3 **Rob:** "So essentially, it was about trade, right?"	☐	☐	☐
4 **Ayman:** "Oh yeah, like Central Asian traders. They had a very important job ... "	☐	☐	☐
5 **Alana:** "Kind of like businesspeople today ... "	☐	☐	☐

Discussion Strategy **Paraphrasing** is putting information that you've heard or read into your own words. We often shorten or simplify information when we paraphrase. You can introduce paraphrases with expressions such as *The general idea was ...* , *What I have is ...* , *Essentially, ...* , and *What she meant was ...* .

C TRY IT In a small group, discuss one or more of these topics. Try to use the discussion strategies you have learned.

- Compare the risks the Silk Road traders faced to the types of risks in travel and business today.
- What does Molly mean by "I guess not that much has changed in the past 2,000 years!"? Do you agree with her?
- During the peak period, Chang'an was an important trade center, and people from many different cultures came into contact. What cities are like this now?

REVIEW your notes

REVIEW Work with a partner. Ask each other questions about the years presented in the lecture. What years and numbers did you write down in your notes? Do you know why they are important? Then consider the reasons why events occurred. For example, why did Rome want to develop routes to China? Try using some of these phrases in your questions:

What happened in ... ?	What is ... ?
When was the (Tang) Dynasty?	What caused ... ?
How many ... ?	Why did ... ?
When did ... ?	

Now add information to this timeline to help you summarize the main ideas of the lecture.

100 BCE → Silk Road begins

_____ – 220 CE → _____ Dynasty _____

_____ → Tang Dynasty _____

_____ → _____ Dynasty _____

_____ CE → trade on Silk Road _____

TIP!
Remember: A timeline is like a "snapshot" of how historic dates and events fit together. It tells the whole story in just a glance!

Now you are ready to take the Unit Test and the Proficiency Assessment.

EXPRESS your ideas

An Impactful Life

In the lecture for this unit, the professor detailed the history of the Silk Road by using a timeline. A timeline details what happened, when it happened, and who or what was involved. Timelines can focus on historical events or people.

Malala Yousafzai with German Chancellor Angela Merkel

TASK **Choose a person you admire who has had a positive impact on history. Then give a short presentation about the person, including a timeline of important events in the person's life. Conclude with key points from your talk.**

Prepare

1 Think of someone you admire, living or dead. This person could be an artist like Michelangelo, a scientist like Stephan Hawking, an activist like Mahatma Gandhi or Malala Yousafzai, an innovator like Steve Jobs, a philanthropist like Bill or Melinda Gates, or anyone who has changed human history. Then do personal or online research to discover three or four events that were significant in shaping that person's life. Make a list of the events.

2 Organize your research into an outline. (Use the example outline to help you.) Order the events chronologically. Add details to your outline as key words and phrases. Remember to include transitions (see p. 51) and a conclusion that reviews key ideas.

3 Work with a partner. Talk about the person you admire and the events you think are important. Compare your outlines and discuss your key ideas. Ask each other questions about your timelines. Talk about how you will conclude your talk.

Practice

4 Practice with your partner. Use the *Unit 6 Presentation Evaluation Form* (in Appendix C) to give each other suggestions to improve your presentations.

5 Practice by yourself. Use the Evaluation Form to evaluate your presentation.

Present

6 Deliver your talk to the class. Remember to glance at your outline occasionally and then look at your audience as you speak. Don't read your presentation. When concluding your presentation, briefly but clearly review your main ideas.

7 When you finish, ask for audience questions: *Are there any questions? How do* **you** *think this person changed history?*

8 Listen to your classmates' presentations.

Evaluate

9 Use the Evaluation Form to evaluate your and your classmates' presentations.

Presentation Strategy: Concluding your presentation

A good conclusion briefly reviews the key information your listeners need to remember from your presentation. Signal your conclusion by using a key phrases such as *In conclusion, we now know …* and *To summarize, we talked about …* . Then rephrase your main ideas. You may also ask your listeners to change their opinion or behavior, think more about the topic, or consider a famous quotation or a very brief audio or video clip that directly relates your points. Be careful: Don't include any new main ideas in your conclusion and never end your presentation by saying *That's all* or *I'm done*.

TOPIC: AN IMPACTFUL LIFE

I Introduction: Main ideas

Transition to 1st event
II Event #1
  A Date
  B Detail
  [optional: **C** Detail]

Transition to 2nd event
III Event #2
  A Date
  B Detail
  [optional: **C** Detail]

Transition to 3rd event
IV Event #3
  A Date
  B Detail
  [optional: **C** Detail]

Transition to 4th event
V Event #4
  A Date
  B Detail
  [optional: **C** Detail]

VI Conclusion: Review of main ideas: Example: *To conclude, we discussed …*

7 Sports Fans

CONNECT to the topic

All over the world there are sports fans who cheer on their favorite teams, or who play sports themselves. Fans celebrate when their favorite teams win. They feel upset when the teams are defeated. However, even with defeat, fans stay loyal to their teams. How would you describe yourself? Are you passionate about sports? Or do you have no interest in sports? What draws people to be sports fans?

A THINK ABOUT IT Take this survey about sports. Check (√) the statements you agree with. Then compare responses with a partner. Give reasons for the statements you don't agree with.

Statement	Agree
• Watching sports is a great way to relax.	☐
• Watching a game is more about having fun with friends or family than who wins.	☐
• Watching sports is a waste of time.	☐
• The competition is what makes watching sports worthwhile.	☐
• I feel like I am part of the game even if I'm only watching it.	☐

B TUNE IN Listen to a talk show interview with sports psychologist Dr. Anika Douglas. With a partner, choose the best answer, based on the interview. More than one answer may be possible.

1 The expression "It's only a game" means: **Don't take it so seriously. / It's not fun. / Your team is not going to win.**

2 Dr. Douglas says that being a sports fan can be good for your **self-esteem / social life / sports team.**

3 The "Sports Spectator Identification Scale" measures **how good your team is / how emotionally involved you are / how lonely you feel.**

4 The host says that he likes to **buy team jerseys / go to his team's games / talk about sports.**

C PAIR WORK Work with a partner. Ask: *Do you know any "super fans"? What do they do? Why are they so interested in their team?*

BUILD your vocabulary

A LISTEN The boldfaced words are from the unit lecture on sports fans. Listen to each sentence. Do you know any synonyms for the boldfaced words?

1 Fans **appreciate** the years of training it takes to be a successful athlete.

2 Fans **bond** with other fans. They share a sense of loss when their team loses and joy when it wins.

3 My sports interests are **broad**—I like everything from ice skating to track and field to rugby.

4 The fans' **commitment** was obvious. They came to every game despite the team's losing record.

5 At an exhibition match, the Olympic team **displayed** its skills to a packed stadium.

6 Trust between the players is an **integral** part of team sports.

7 The desire to be part of a community **motivates** some people to become sports fans.

8 The rivalry between the two teams was **ongoing**, lasting many years.

9 Winning the championship game **reinforced** the team's sense of pride.

10 The fans were upbeat, their **self-esteem** unaffected by the team's loss.

B TRY IT Match each boldfaced word with its definition.

____	**1 appreciate**	**a**	dedication to something
____	**2 bond**	**b**	clearly show a feeling, attitude, quality
____	**3 broad**	**c**	develop a special relationship
____	**4 commitment**	**d**	value the good qualities of something or someone
____	**5 display**	**e**	strengthen
____	**6 integral**	**f**	the feeling that you deserve to be liked or admired
____	**7 motivate**	**g**	continuing
____	**8 ongoing**	**h**	fundamental, essential
____	**9 reinforce**	**i**	general, main
____	**10 self-esteem**	**j**	entice or encourage someone to do something

C PAIR WORK Work with a partner. Read the sentences in Column A and discuss the meanings of the boldfaced phrases. Then read sentences 1–5 aloud as your partner fills in the blanks in Column B. Switch roles for 6–10.

COLUMN A

1 The friends had different **motivations for** being sports fans.

2 The whole country enjoyed the **performance of** the Olympic athletes.

3 Not everyone is **interested in** sports to the same degree.

4 I like to analyze the **strategy of** the team and try to figure out their next play.

5 The team fought to get an **advantage over** their opponent.

6 Many fans experience a **sense of** belonging as they watch their favorite team.

7 The theory was **originated by** two psychologists a while back.

8 Sports fans enjoy **affiliating with** their team as well as with other fans.

9 One interesting **aspect of** fan affiliation is a sense of loyalty.

10 Fans often **identify with** particular players on their favorite teams.

COLUMN B

1 The friends had different **motivations** _____ being sports fans.

2 The whole country enjoyed the **performance** _____ the Olympic athletes.

3 Not everyone is **interested** _____ sports to the same degree.

4 I like to analyze the **strategy** _____ the team and try to figure out their next play.

5 The team fought to get an **advantage** _____ their opponent.

6 Many fans experience a **sense** _____ belonging as they watch their favorite team.

7 The theory was **originated** _____ two psychologists a while back.

8 Sports fans enjoy **affiliating** _____ their team as well as with other fans.

9 One interesting **aspect** _____ fan affiliation is a sense of loyalty.

10 Fans often **identify** _____ particular players on their favorite teams.

FOCUS your attention

Enumerating

A speaker often provides organizational cues to help you understand the ideas you hear. One way a speaker does this is by enumerating and then repeating a key word or phrase. The speaker does this to provide a framework to make it easier for you to understand how the ideas are connected. The speaker then presents one characteristic at a time, and signals what's next by **stating a new number** and **repeating the key word or phrase.**

NUMBER and REPETITION CUES

Today I'm going to talk about **three characteristics** of successful athletes.

Characteristic 1: Successful athletes are dedicated ...

Characteristic 2: Successful athlete are focused ...

Characteristic 3: Successful athlete are not afraid of failure ...

These notes are from a lecture organized with numbers and a list of ideas, signaled by a repeated key word (*Characteristic*).

Successful Athletes Characteristics	Examples / details
1) dedicated	practice regularly, disciplined
2) focused	determined, don't give up
3) aren't afraid of failure	feel they can always improve

A TRY IT Listen to an excerpt from a class lecture about sports fans. What numbers, repeated key phrase, and ideas do you hear? Take notes in a chart.

B PAIR WORK Compare notes with a partner.

WATCH the lecture

Professor Colin Edwards

A THINK ABOUT IT You are about to watch the unit lecture on sports fans. In your opinion, why are people sports fans?

_____

_____

B LISTEN FOR MAIN IDEAS Close your book. Watch the lecture and take notes.

C CHECK YOUR UNDERSTANDING Use your notes. Answer the questions, based on the lecture. Circle *a*, *b*, or *c*.

1 What is the lecture mainly about?

   a the reasons people play sports
   b the reasons people become sports fans
   c the reasons people like competition

2 In what order does the speaker present the topics?

   a motivations, social media, Social Identity Theory
   b social media, Social Identity Theory, motivations
   c motivations, Social Identity Theory, social media

3 What is Social Identity Theory mainly about?

   a the idea that people behave in certain ways in order to increase their social status
   b the idea that people do things to increase their self-esteem
   c the idea that people are interested in competition

4 What is the main reason people become fans?

   a to understand how to be better at sports
   b to follow the players' stories
   c to feel part of a community

5 Which of the following statements would the speaker disagree with?

   a Being a fan fulfills an important human need.
   b Humans have a drive to belong to a group.
   c Watching sports is essentially a waste of time.

D LISTEN FOR DETAILS Close your book. Watch the lecture again. Add details to your notes and correct any mistakes.

E **CHECK YOUR UNDERSTANDING** Use your notes. Complete the sentences, based on the lecture.

analyze	competition	bond	drama	motivation

1 There is a deeper social _____ for being a sports fan than just entertainment.

2 The third motivation for fans is to follow the _____ and personal stories of the players.

3 As fans watch, they become involved and feel they are actually in the _____ .

4 The fourth motivation is that fans like to _____ the strategy of the different teams.

5 The fifth motivation is to _____ with others who share a common interest.

team colors	loyal	national	social media	self-identify

6 Fans feel part of a _____ community when their country wins an Olympic medal.

7 Wearing _____ is one way that fans show their affiliation with the team.

8 A team's successes and failures become part of a sports fan's _____ .

9 Out of dedication to the group, fans remain _____ to the team even when it loses.

10 _____ makes it easy for fans to share their commitment to the team.

HEAR the language

Linked Sounds

Speakers often **link** the final sound of one word to the first sound of the next word. This can produce a vowel-like sound called a glide. Linking can make two, three, or even four words sound like one word. This is a natural part of English speech because it helps keep the rhythm of the sentences.

> **EXAMPLES**
>
> Glide sound /w/: *to a* → *towa*   Glide sound /y/: *see it* → *seeyit*

A LISTEN Listen and complete the statements and questions from the lecture. Complete the words you hear.

1 I don't _____ w a _____ you, but I spent the entire weekend watching World Cup matches.

2 And while some people think of sports as just _____ f_____ n

i_____, social psychologists _____ ve _____

wider view.

3 Many modern social psychologists say that watching sports—and identifying _____ th

_____ particular player or team—_____ s _____ n

i_____ human need.

4 _____ s i_____ the need to belong _____ o

_____ group and feel a _____ se o_____

self-esteem.

5 Games are interesting _____ y _____ f _____ y

i_____ some kind of problem solving and decision making.

6 How do they try to _____ t _____ n a_____ over

their opponents?

7 For example, at the Olympics, _____ g _____

s_____ fan is a way for people to feel _____ d

a_____ _____ nation.

8 By associating or affiliating with a team—by wearing team colors or by going to games and

tracking _____ s a_____ losses—fans feel that they

_____ re _____ n i_____ part of something.

9 _____ s o_____ exchange keeps _____ s

i_____ in the team community.

10 _____ e a_____ l h_____ ve

_____ human drive to be part of a group and to feel _____ d

a_____ t o_____ .

B PAIR WORK Work with a partner. Take turns saying the sentences. Pay attention to the linking.

TALK about the topic

Agreeing

A FOLLOW THE DISCUSSION Watch as the students talk about sports fans. Read each comment. Then check (✓) the student who makes the comment.

Ben   Kenzie   Hugh   Shelley

	Ben	Kenzie	Hugh	Shelley
1 "I think people follow sports for the competition."	☐	☐	☐	☐
2 "I admit I go for the drama ... how they face challenges."	☐	☐	☐	☐
3 "There's also the fun of analyzing the strategy."	☐	☐	☐	☐
4 "I wouldn't say watching sports increases my self-esteem."	☐	☐	☐	☐

B LEARN THE STRATEGIES Watch the discussion again. Listen closely for the comments. Then check (✓) the discussion strategy the student uses.

	Agreeing	Asking for clarification or confirmation	Asking for opinions or ideas
1 Ben: "What are the main reasons people watch sports?"	☐	☐	☐
2 Ben: "Not a big sports fan?"	☐	☐	☐
3 Hugh: "Yeah, me, too."	☐	☐	☐
4 Hugh: "Yeah, yeah."	☐	☐	☐
5 Shelley: "What does that mean, 'community'?"	☐	☐	☐

Discussion Strategy Observe a group discussion and you're likely to hear **expressions of agreement** like *Uh-huh, Right, Yes, I agree, Exactly, Sure, Yeah*, and *No doubt*. Agreeing is an important way to build understanding with another speaker. Even if you only agree with part of what the speaker says, you can show "partial agreement." For example: *I agree with what you said about ... .*

C TRY IT In a small group, discuss one or more of these topics. Try to use the discussion strategies you have learned.

- Based on your own experiences, what types of activities create a sense of community?
- Do you agree that people are sports fans out of a human drive to be part of a community?
- Do you belong to any online communities? Do you feel it's the same as or different from face-to-face communities you belong to?

REVIEW your notes

REVIEW With a partner, review the main ideas of the lecture. Use your notes. Paraphrase and clarify the ideas. Here are some expressions you can use:

> *Basically, ...*
> *In a nutshell, ...*
> *To paraphrase / sum up what the lecturer said, ...*
> *I'm not sure I understand. Are you saying ... ?*
> *It sounds like you are saying ... Does that mean ... ?*
> *You mentioned ... Does that mean ... ?*
> *Can you give me some examples of what you mean by ... ?*

Now compare the organization in your notes. Then compare with and complete those below.

Five motivations for being sports fans:

1st motivation is ...

2nd motivation is ...

3rd motivation is ...

4th motivation is ...

5th motivation is ...

Social Identity Theory

Theory says:

Self-esteem includes:

Theory applied to sports fans:

Use of social media

Conclusion:

Human drive / group identity

TIP!

As you learned in Unit 6, *to paraphrase* means to say something in your own words. You can also paraphrase what someone else has said to make sure you have understood the information correctly.

Now you are ready to take the Unit Test and the Proficiency Assessment.

EXPRESS your ideas

A Special Passion

In this unit, the lecturer talked about the love of sports and five motivations for being a sports fan. Which motivations do you think explain why you or someone you know enjoys a particular sport or activity?

TASK Learn about a classmate's interest in a sport or activity. Then give a short presentation about your findings. Use an attention-getting opener.

Prepare

1 Interview a classmate about a sport or activity he or she is passionate about. Discuss what motivates him or her to love the sport or activity. Ask a lot of "why" questions.

2 Make a list of his or her motivations. Why does he or she love the sport or activity? Review your lecture notes for the reasons people follow sports.

3 Organize your interview notes into an outline. (Use the example outline to help you.) Use your classmate's motivations to create the main points of your outline. In the outline, highlight two of the strongest motivations. Add details to your outline as key words and phrases. Write transition words or phrases between the main points. Create an attention-getting opener.

4 Work with a partner. Compare your outlines. Talk first about the effectiveness of your attention-getting opener. Then discuss the motivations. Ask each other questions.

Practice

5 Practice with your partner. Did your attention-getting opener immediately "catch" your partner's interest? Did you cover the motivations well? Use the *Unit 7 Presentation Evaluation Form* (in Appendix C) to give each other suggestions to improve your presentations.

Present

6 Deliver your presentation to the class. Try to speak naturally and confidently.

7 When you finish, ask for audience questions: *Does anyone have a question about [classmate's name]'s motivations for [his / her] love of the sport / activity?*

8 Listen to your classmates' presentations.

Evaluate

9 Use the Evaluation Form to evaluate your and your classmates' presentations. Give comments that will encourage your classmates to improve!

Presentation Strategy: Using an attention-getting opener

To capture your listeners' attention immediately, start your presentation with an attention-getting opener. Like a "hook" to catch a fish, this initial surprising or amusing question, statement, or quote doesn't state your topic but "catches" your audience by making them curious about what you will say next. For example, you could ask:

Do you know what [name] really enjoys and why?

What do you think [name] would love to do on a free Saturday?

Imagine next Saturday is a great day. What do you think [name] will do?

TOPIC: A SPECIAL PASSION

Attention-getting opener

I Introduction
  A Classmate's sport or activity
  B Main ideas: 2–3 motivations

Transition to motivation #1: "His / Her first motivation is …"
II Motivation #1
  A Detail
  B Detail

Transition to motivation #2
III Motivation #2
  A Detail
  B Detail

Transition to conclusion
IV Conclusion

8 Frank Gehry

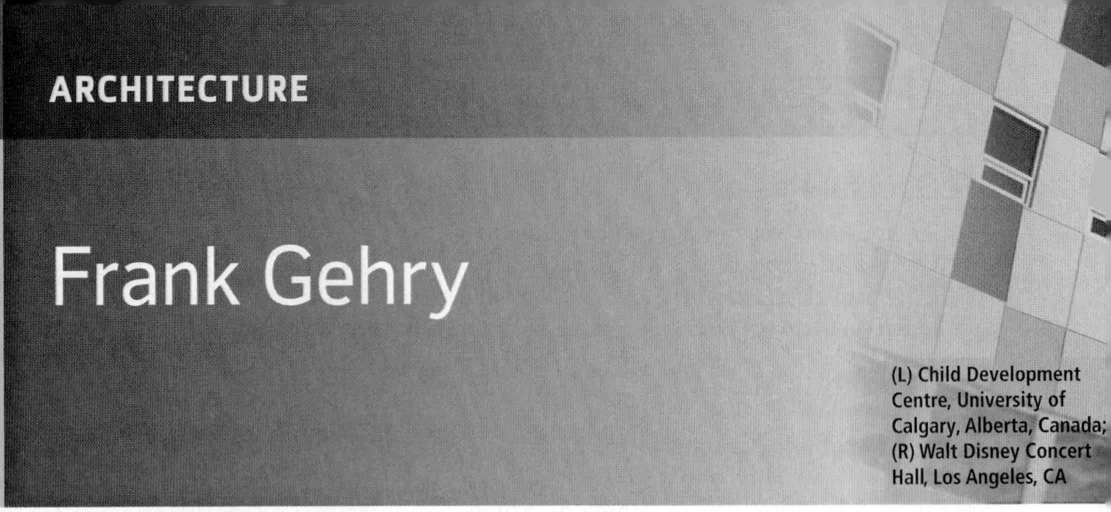

(L) Child Development Centre, University of Calgary, Alberta, Canada; (R) Walt Disney Concert Hall, Los Angeles, CA

CONNECT to the topic

Architecture draws on many fields: art, engineering, mathematics, environmental studies, even philosophy. Long ago, the Roman architect Vitruvius said a building must be strong, functional, and beautiful. These three principles of architecture still guide us today. What makes a building beautiful?

A THINK ABOUT IT Look at the buildings pictured above and consider these questions. Then share responses with a partner.

- What aspects of each building's design do you like or dislike?
- What do you think each building is used for?
- What features make each seem strong enough to last a long time?

B TUNE IN Listen to a conversation between Max, a prospective student, and Leila, a campus guide. Then work with a partner to answer the questions, based on the conversation.

1 What is Leila's opinion of the Child Development Centre building?

_____

2 What is the main reason Max doesn't like the building?

_____

3 Leila says, "Everyone's ideas about that vary." What does she mean?

_____

C PAIR WORK Work with a partner. Ask: _What is your favorite modern building? What is your favorite old or historical building? Why do you like these structures? What are some current trends in the design of buildings?_

BUILD your vocabulary

A LISTEN The boldfaced words are from the unit lecture on architect Frank Gehry. Listen to each sentence. Then match the meaning to the boldfaced word.

_____ 1 Architects consider the **aesthetics** of the buildings they design. They want people to find the buildings not only beautiful to look at but also enjoyable to be inside.

_____ 2 The **foundation** of architecture today is based on the fundamentals of the past.

_____ 3 The architect Frank Gehry is **inspirational**. He pushes other architects to explore new ideas.

_____ 4 The **intended use** or purpose of a mall is a place to shop. For example, a café's intended use is as a place to eat.

_____ 5 To say a building is structurally **sound** means that it is built to last a long time.

    a causing others to do or produce something
    b the basis; the ideas that support something
    c reason for the building
    d artistic value
    e in good condition; strong

_____ 6 Frank Gehry is noteworthy because of his **dynamic** style. His designs are very creative and unusual.

_____ 7 A building must serve the needs and purposes of the people who use it. If the building does this, then the architect has **met the objective**.

_____ 8 Aesthetics is a difficult **principle** to agree on because people have their own taste.

_____ 9 Frank Gehry's designs often use irregular angles. It's important to **stress**, however, that the designs are still structurally sound.

_____ 10 Frank Gehry was resourceful because he liked to **utilize** chain-link fence, plywood, sheet metal, and other building materials that were easily available to him.

    f achieved the goal
    g rule or set of ideas
    h use something effectively
    i exciting; interesting; full of energy
    j emphasize

B PAIR WORK Work with a partner. Notice the boldfaced words. Take turns completing each sentence with the correct form of the word. Read the completed sentences aloud. Review any words you don't understand.

aesthetic	aesthetically	aesthetics

1 One of the basic **principles of** architecture is to consider the _____ of a building—for example the materials, lighting, and shape.

2 One _____ **consideration of** a structure's design is shape. The shape of the Arc de Triomphe in Paris, for example, is very strong and commanding. It is difficult to design a structure that is _____ **pleasing to** everyone.

distinct	distinguish

3 Frank Gehry has a _____ style, especially his **use of** irregular shapes.

4 It's not difficult to _____ his work **from that of** other architects.

innovation	innovative	innovator

5 Frank Gehry is considered an _____ . Trying new ideas was **at the foundation of** his designs.

6 An _____ architect doesn't follow traditional **styles of** building design.

7 A fairly recent _____ in architecture includes an **emphasis on** "going green," which means designing with the environment in mind.

sculptor	sculpture

8 The Fish Dance restaurant in Kobe, Japan, **looks like** a gigantic _____ of a fish.

9 I can't remember the name of the _____ , but I liked how she **experimented with** shapes.

FOCUS your attention

Emphasis

During a lecture, you hear a lot of information quickly. Lecturers will often use signal phrases or emphasize words to focus your attention on important information. If they want to check in to see if you are following along, lecturers may cue you with questions.

SIGNALING EMPHASIS	CHECKING IN
To highlight what I've said so far ...	*Is everyone clear on this?*
I want to emphasize that ...	*Is this clear?*
I want to stress ...	*Are there any questions?*
It's important to understand ...	*Are you with me?*
The fundamental point is ...	
What I'm saying is ...	

Say you hear this: *I want to stress that architecture is both an art and a science ... . There are many factors to consider in the design of a building ... . Are you with me?* Your notes might look like this:

Architecture = <u>an art and a science</u>
When designing a bldg: <u>many factors to consider</u>

🔊 **A TRY IT** Listen to an excerpt from an architecture class. Which signal phrases and cues does the speaker use? Take notes. Underline the important information.

B PAIR WORK Compare notes with a partner.

WATCH the lecture

A THINK ABOUT IT You are about to watch the unit lecture on Frank Gehry. Check (√) the top three considerations you think an architect should keep in mind when designing a building.

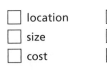

Professor Zachary Boyd

- ☐ location
- ☐ size
- ☐ cost
- ☐ colors
- ☐ energy use
- ☐ number of windows
- ☐ use of recycled or environmentally responsible materials

B LISTEN FOR MAIN IDEAS Close your book. Watch the lecture and take notes.

C CHECK YOUR UNDERSTANDING Use your notes. Answer the questions, based on the lecture. Circle *a*, *b*, or *c*.

1 How is architecture both a science and an art?

  a Buildings must look nice from the outside and the inside.
  b Buildings must be strong and beautiful.
  c Buildings must protect people from bad weather.

2 Why does the professor mention Vitruvius?

  a to show that the principles of architecture change
  b to show that Gehry's work is based on principles from long ago
  c to show how styles in architecture change

3 What aspect of Gehry's work does the lecture mainly focus on?

  a his building style in the 1970s
  b examples of his work around the world
  c his distinctive style

4 Why does Gehry use bright, bold colors?

  a He wants to be playful.
  b He's concerned about the environment.
  c He wants his buildings to be strong.

5 Why did Gehry develop his dynamic style?

  a He liked to experiment with building houses.
  b Other architects didn't agree with his ideas.
  c Traditional architecture didn't allow him to be creative enough.

6 What is the main reason the professor likes Gehry?

  a because Gehry understands traditional values in architecture
  b because Gehry is innovative and resourceful
  c because Gehry has designed many different buildings

The Vitra Design Museum, Weil am Rhein, Germany

D LISTEN FOR DETAILS Close your book. Watch the lecture again. Add details to your notes and correct any mistakes.

E CHECK YOUR UNDERSTANDING Use your notes. Decide if the statements are *T* (true) or *F* (false), based on the lecture. Correct any false statements.

_____ **1** Designing buildings is both an art and a science.

_____ **2** An example of a building being sound is one that protects people from bad weather.

_____ **3** The professor says that the intended use of a library is as a place to learn.

_____ **4** Everyone agrees on aesthetics because styles in architecture don't change much.

_____ **5** Plywood and sheet metal are examples of simple building materials Gehry used in the 1970s.

_____ **6** The main reason Gehry used chain-link fence was that he thought it was beautiful.

_____ **7** The professor is worried that the Vitra Design Museum in Germany might fall down because it doesn't look sound.

_____ **8** Gehry used irregular shapes and angles to see what was possible from an engineering standpoint.

_____ **9** The professor believes Gehry thinks more like an engineer than an artist.

_____ **10** Gehry thinks of buildings as sculptures that people interact with.

HEAR the language

Intonation

In statements, a speaker's **intonation** rises to signal new information or important words. It falls to signal the end of an information unit—usually the last word of a sentence.

In *yes-no* questions, a speaker's intonation typically falls and then rises at the end. In *wh-* questions, on the other hand, a speaker's intonation rises and then falls at the end.

EXAMPLES

Are you ready?
↓   ↑

Is that the answer?
↓   ↑

When will you be ready?
↑   ↓

What is the answer?
↑   ↓

A LISTEN Listen and complete the statements and questions from the lecture. Write the missing words. Circle ↑ or ↓ to indicate whether the intonation rises or falls at the end of the word.

1 It's a _____ _____ building near the _____ .
   ↑↓   ↑↓   ↑↓

2 We use science to make _____ that the building is _____ .
                          ↑↓   ↑↓

3 He said that a building must have _____ fundamental _____ .
                                     ↑↓   ↑↓

4 _____ , a building must meet its intended _____ .
   ↑↓   ↑↓

5 What type of design is best for both _____ and _____ ?
                                        ↑↓   ↑↓

6 Is it _____ ? Will it last a _____ _____ ?
         ↑↓   ↑↓   ↑↓

7 Styles in architecture _____ , like with _____ or _____ .
                          ↑↓   ↑↓   ↑↓

8 Have any of you _____ his _____ ?
                   ↑↓   ↑↓

9 Specifically, how can we _____ his _____ ?
                            ↑↓   ↑↓

10 I can think of three words: _____ , _____ , and _____ .
                                ↑↓   ↑↓   ↑↓

B PAIR WORK Work with a partner. Take turns saying the sentences. Pay attention to the intonation.

TALK about the topic

Acknowledging a Point

A FOLLOW THE DISCUSSION Watch as the students talk about Frank Gehry. Read each opinion. Then check (✓) who disagrees with it.

Michael   Yhinny   May   Qiang

	Michael	Yhinny	May	Qiang
1 Frank Gehry is one of the greatest architects ever.	☐	☐	☐	☐
2 Frank Gehry will be forgotten by history.	☐	☐	☐	☐
3 Frank Gehry's engineering abilities are put to good use.	☐	☐	☐	☐
4 I'm a Frank Gehry enthusiast.	☐	☐	☐	☐

B LEARN THE STRATEGIES Watch the discussion again. Listen closely for the comments. Then check (✓) the discussion strategy the student uses. More than one answer may be correct.

	Acknowledging a point	Asking for opinions or ideas	Disagreeing
1 Yhinny: "What? I wouldn't say that."	☐	☐	☐
2 Michael: "I mean, I hate to disagree, but … "	☐	☐	☐
3 May: "OK, then what would you say about his engineering abilities—can you say he's noteworthy for that?"	☐	☐	☐
4 Michael: "OK, sure, I can see that. But … ."	☐	☐	☐
5 Michael: "Why doesn't he put those abilities to use in a more practical way? Like building bridges?"	☐	☐	☐

Discussion Strategy Even if you disagree with someone, you may **acknowledge** a small part of that person's argument. Typical expressions of acknowledgement include *I see what you mean, but … , I can see that, but … ,* and *That's true, however … .*

C TRY IT In a small group, discuss one or more of these topics. Try to use the discussion strategies you have learned.

- Yhinny says that Frank Gehry's buildings are all over the world. What is her point?
- Michael suggests that someone like Frank Gehry should use his skills in practical ways like designing bridges rather than designing aesthetically pleasing buildings. Do you agree?
- Some say Frank Gehry doesn't pay enough attention to the environment. Would these students agree with this criticism? Would you?

REVIEW your notes

REVIEW Work with a partner to complete the outline. Use your notes. Then retell the main ideas of the lecture in your own words.

I. 3 principles from Vitruvius: Ex.'s / Details:

    A

    B

    C

II. 3 features of Gehry's style: Ex.'s / Details:

    A

    B

    C

III. Ex.'s of his work:

IV. Reason(s) Gehry developed his style:

V. Reason(s) Professor Boyd likes Gehry:

> **TIP!**
> When a speaker "checks in," this is your chance to clarify anything you don't understand.

🔊 **Now you are ready to take the Unit Test and the Proficiency Assessment.**

EXPRESS your ideas

A Beautiful Building

In this unit, the lecturer discussed three key architectural characteristics: intended use, strength, and beauty. Architects such as Frank Gehry include innovation while following these principles. There are buildings all over the world that meet these criteria.

St. Basil's Cathedral, Moscow, Russia

TASK Research a building that interests you and fulfills the three key architectural characteristics while displaying creativity. Then give a short presentation about your findings. Use visual aids.

Prepare

1 Choose a building you like. It might be your house, your apartment building, your school, or a famous building such as the Burj Khalifa in Dubai, St Basil's Cathedral in Russia, or the Sidney Opera House in Australia. Go online to research the building. How does it meet its intended use? How is it beautiful? How is it innovative or playful? Find pictures that show these characteristics.

2 Organize your research into an outline. (Use the example outline to help you.) Use your list of characteristics as your main ideas. Use key words and short phrases to add details to your outline. Use pictures to support your main ideas or details. Below these pictures, include the source information. Remember to begin with an attention-getter and then give your main ideas. Don't forget to use transitions to introduce new main ideas and a conclusion that reviews those main points.

3 Work with a partner. Take turns talking about your buildings' characteristics. Compare your outlines and discuss your key ideas. Use your pictures to support your ideas.

Practice

4 Practice with your partner. Did you follow the order of ideas in your outline? Did you look at your partner while you showed your visual aids? Use the *Unit 8 Presentation Evaluation Form* (in Appendix C) to give each other suggestions to improve your presentations.

5 Practice by yourself. Record your presentation or practice in front of a mirror.

Present

6 Deliver your presentation to the class. For your conclusion, review your main ideas.

7 When you finish, ask for audience questions. After your conclusion ask: *Are there any questions? Would you like me go over any characteristics of this building again?*

8 Listen to your classmates' presentations.

Evaluate

9 Use the Evaluation Form to evaluate your and your classmates' presentations. Be supportive: Give comments that will encourage your classmates to improve!

Presentation Strategy: Presenting with visual aids

Colorful and creative visual aids help your audience understand and remember your ideas. When selecting a visual aid, be sure to use an object, picture, or slide that is clear, uncomplicated, and large enough for everyone to see. If you include an image taken from the Internet or a printed publication, include the source information (for example, the url: www.fallingwater.org) below the picture. Finally, remember to look at your audience, not your visual aid!

TOPIC: A BEAUTIFUL BUILDING

Attention-getting opener
 I Introduction: Main ideas

Transition to characteristic #1
 II Intended use *Visual aid*
   A Detail (purpose built)
   B Detail (past use)
   C Detail (current use)

Transition to characteristic #2
 III Beauty *Visual aid*
   A Detail #1
   B Detail #2
   [*optional:* **C** Detail #3]

Transition to characteristic #3
 IV Innovative or Playful *Visual aid*
   A Detail #1
   B Detail #2
   [*optional:* **C** Detail #3]

 V Conclusion: Review of main ideas

9 Global Epidemic

CONNECT to the topic

What does it take to be healthy? Good food? Protection from disease? Exercise? Clean water and air? Public health officials are concerned about your health as well as that of the entire community. They look at ways to prevent diseases from spreading and to promote health so that everyone can live healthier lives.

A THINK ABOUT IT Consider these questions about health. Then compare responses with a partner.

- Are you a "healthy" person? What do you do to stay healthy?
- Are you an "active" person? How much exercise do you get each week?
- Do you generally "eat healthy"? What are your favorite foods?

B TUNE IN Listen to a conversation between a wellness counselor and Tomas, a client. Then answer the questions, based on the conversation. Compare answers with a partner.

1 What is Tomas's goal?

_____

2 What does the counselor recommend?

_____

3 What do they agree to do?

_____

C PAIR WORK Work with a partner. Ask: *What does the phrase "healthy lifestyle" mean to you? What behaviors are healthy and unhealthy? How much do your family and friends influence the choices you make?*

LEARNING OUTCOMES

In this unit you will:

- practice using symbols and abbreviations in your notes
- restate the main ideas of a public health lecture
- note details from a public health lecture
- identify and practice emphasizing words
- recognize and practice strategies for offering a fact or example
- review and summarize your lecture notes to prepare for the unit test
- give a presentation about making healthy changes, using nonverbal communication

BUILD your vocabulary

A LISTEN The boldfaced words are from the unit lecture on a global epidemic. Listen to each sentence. Then match the meaning to the boldfaced word.

_____ **1** We know **approximately** how many people are obese. We don't have exact figures.

_____ **2** People who regularly consume **excess** calories gain weight.

_____ **3** Health care workers **witness** many overweight patients at the clinics.

a observe	**b** generally	**c** too many

_____ **4** The school plans to **adopt** a new schedule. They want to give students time to exercise.

_____ **5** People who are **affluent** have extra money to spend on entertainment and travel.

_____ **6** The **guidelines** for healthy eating include how many vegetables to eat daily.

d start to use	**e** suggested rules	**f** wealthy

_____ **7** There are several factors that **contribute to** the problem, not just one.

_____ **8** The companies decided to **implement** nutrition classes for employees.

_____ **9** The man was too busy to exercise. This had a **negative** impact on his health.

_____ **10** There has been a **shift** in what people prefer to eat.

g cause	**h** begin to make happen	**i** major change	**j** harmful

B PAIR WORK Work with a partner. Read the sentences in Column A and discuss the meanings of the boldfaced phrases. Then read sentences 1–5 aloud as your partner fills in the blanks in Column B. Switch roles for 6–10.

COLUMN A	COLUMN B
1 There's a **formula for** measuring obesity.	**1** There's a **formula** _____ measuring obesity.
2 The **occurrence of** obesity is increasing.	**2** The **occurrence** _____ obesity is increasing.
3 Some people are **putting on weight at** an alarming rate.	**3** Some people are **putting on weight** _____ an alarming rate.
4 The **percentage of** obese people is likely to increase.	**4** The **percentage** _____ obese people is likely to increase.
5 What are the **causes of** this epidemic?	**5** What are the **causes** _____ this epidemic?
6 The **role of** food is changing.	**6** The **role** _____ food is changing.
7 The guidelines suggest **a minimum of** 30 minutes of exercise each day.	**7** The guidelines suggest **a minimum** _____ 30 minutes of exercise each day.
8 The food **standards in** schools are changing.	**8** The food **standards** _____ schools are changing.
9 Treatment must **focus on** several factors.	**9** Treatment must **focus** _____ several factors.
10 A public health worker is **assigned to** a family.	**10** A public health worker is **assigned** _____ a family.

FOCUS your attention

Symbols and Abbreviations

As you listen to a lecture, it's important to be able to take notes quickly. One helpful technique is to use symbols and abbreviations. You can create your own, or you can use standard ones.

SYMBOL OR ABBREVIATION	MEANING
eg. or ex.	for example ("exempli gratia" is Latin for "for example")
etc.	additional persons or things ("et cetera" is Latin for "and other things")
i.e.	in other words ("id est" is Latin for "that is")
&	and
@	at
↑	increase
↓	decrease
#	amount OR number of
=	is OR equals
≠	isn't OR doesn't equal
x	number of times (2x)
→	causes OR results in
?	question

Say you hear this: *It's a global epidemic—for example, there's an increase in the number of people who are obese.* Your notes might look like this:

Global epidemic; e.g., ↑ # people obese

🔊 **A TRY IT** Listen to an excerpt from a public health conference. Take notes using symbols and abbreviations.

B PAIR WORK Compare notes with a partner. What symbols and abbreviations did you use?

WATCH the lecture

Professor Julian Young

A THINK ABOUT IT You are about to watch the unit lecture on obesity as a global epidemic. What are possible reasons the speaker is calling obesity an epidemic?

_____

_____

B LISTEN FOR MAIN IDEAS Close your book. Watch the lecture and take notes.

C CHECK YOUR UNDERSTANDING Use your notes. Answer the questions, based on the lecture. Circle *a*, *b*, or *c*.

1 What's the lecture mainly about?

   a the countries affected by obesity
   b different types of epidemics in the world today
   c the causes of the obesity epidemic

2 According to the lecture, why is obesity considered an epidemic?

   a It's impossible to cure.
   b It's spreading worldwide.
   c It's affecting children.

3 What does the professor mean when he says obesity is no longer just "a disease of affluence"?

   a It is affecting wealthy people.
   b It is affecting people from all income levels.
   c It is affecting many children.

4 The professor says "increased use of technology for work and leisure, less physical activity, greater use of cars, growing access to ... fast food." What is he describing?

   a the reasons that modern lifestyles have made our lives more enjoyable
   b the goals of developing countries to reach the standards of developed countries
   c the features of the modern lifestyle that are causing the epidemic

5 What is the professor's general attitude toward a successful treatment program?

   a It must include group support.
   b It should aim to eliminate technology from our lives.
   c It should not involve the workplace.

6 What can be inferred from the professor saying the epidemic is a "call to action"?

   a He thinks it's difficult to stay healthy.
   b He thinks neighborhood classes are helpful.
   c He thinks it's a serious public health problem.

D LISTEN FOR DETAILS Close your book. Watch the lecture again. Add details to your notes and correct any mistakes.

E CHECK YOUR UNDERSTANDING Use your notes. Decide if the sentences are *T* (*true*) or *F* (*false*), based on the lecture. Correct any false statements.

_____ **1** Obesity is a health condition in which someone has an excess amount of body fat.

_____ **2** A Body Mass Index of 30 is considered normal.

_____ **3** Approximately 300 million adults worldwide are obese.

_____ **4** The rate of increase of obesity in children is greater in developed countries than in developing countries.

_____ **5** According to the professor, a modern lifestyle includes easy access to inexpensive, fast foods.

_____ **6** A modern lifestyle involves more use of technology and less physical activity.

_____ **7** The research shows that shared meal times help people have better nutrition.

_____ **8** Adults need at least 60 minutes of physical activity a day to be healthy.

_____ **9** In Nigeria, neighborhood nutrition classes have been implemented.

_____ **10** "Keep Moving" is an example of a program designed to provide group support.

HEAR the language

Emphasized Words

English speakers sometimes **emphasize** a word or phrase that is not usually emphasized. This changes the expected rhythm of the sentence and gets the listener's attention.

> **EXAMPLE**
> And, *surprisingly*, the rate of increase for **children** in these economically developing countries is 30 percent **greater** than in developed countries.

A LISTEN Listen to the statements and questions from the lecture. Circle the word the professor emphasizes most in each underlined phrase. Some items have two words.

1 Today, we're going to talk about another kind of epidemic—one that is non-infectious. This is the epidemic of obesity, which is now officially a global health problem.

2 According to the W-H-O, worldwide obesity has more than doubled in the past 35 years.

3 Today, approximately 600 million adults are considered obese, and obesity in children has increased sharply.

4 So, that's what's going on: The world is putting on weight at an alarming rate.

5 Increasingly, we're witnessing the occurrence of obesity all over the world, with middle- and low-income people.

6 The food people prefer is changing. We now see fast food replacing traditional food in many parts of the world.

7 We're also seeing a behavioral shift. The role of food is changing.

8 In short, we're seeing that as countries develop economically, people make lifestyle changes that seem like improvements, but actually have a negative impact on their health.

9 So, we know obesity is a growing global epidemic. And we also know from research that any successful obesity treatment program must have a three-level approach.

10 So, what can and are public health workers doing to respond to this epidemic?

B PAIR WORK Work with a partner. Take turns saying the sentences. Pay attention to word emphasis and how it affects the rhythm of the sentence.

TALK about the topic

Offering a Fact or Example

A FOLLOW THE DISCUSSION Watch as the students talk about the lecture. Read each comment. Then check (√) the student who makes the comment.

Kenzie   Hugh   Shelley   Ben

	Kenzie	Hugh	Shelley	Ben
1 "If everyone is ready, we can begin."	☐	☐	☐	☐
2 "Well, I'd never thought about it as an *epidemic*, ... but ... ."	☐	☐	☐	☐
3 "I've always thought of obesity as more of a problem in countries like the US."	☐	☐	☐	☐
4 "So, wait, is that an example of food as entertainment?"	☐	☐	☐	☐

B LEARN THE STRATEGIES Watch the discussion again. Listen closely for the comments. Then check (√) the discussion strategy the student uses.

	Asking for opinions or ideas	Offering a fact or example	Paraphrasing
1 Kenzie: "What did everyone think about calling obesity a global epidemic?"	☐	☐	☐
2 Shelley: "To me, the big concern is the rate of increase in developing countries ... ."	☐	☐	☐
3 Ben: "For instance, my friends and I, we'll cook together rather than ordering a pizza ... ."	☐	☐	☐
4 Hugh: "Food as entertainment was meant in a negative way."	☐	☐	☐

Discussion Strategy By **offering a fact or example**, you can make a topic more concrete. This can make the topic not only more understandable, but also more memorable. Personal experiences (*In my experience ...*), observations (*I've noticed ...*) and media (*I just read this article about ...*) are a few ways you can begin.

C TRY IT In a small group, discuss one or more of these topics. Try to use the discussion strategies you have learned.

- Do you agree that obesity should be called an epidemic?
- What examples of changes in lifestyles have you noticed in your community?
- Shelley says, "Every kid now wants to play video games and eat snacks ... ." Do you agree with this?

REVIEW your notes

REVIEW With a partner, use the following questions to retell the main ideas from the lecture. Use your notes. As you listen to your partner, complete the notes below.

- Why is obesity being called a global epidemic?
- What is the WHO definition of obesity?
- In what type of countries is the rate of increase faster?
- What is the main reason for this increase?
- What are examples of lifestyle changes?
- What must a successful treatment program focus on?
- What are examples of these approaches?

Reason obesity = global epidemic:

WHO definition of obesity:

Countries affected:

Reasons for ↑

Ex. lifestyle changes

Successful treatment programs
    characteristics:

    ex:

> **TIP!**
>
> As you review the lecture, say the words for the symbols and abbreviations you used in your notes to help capture the key information.

Now check over your notes. Make sure they are complete and clear.
Ask yourself: *Would I be able to recall the key ideas of the lecture later using these notes?* Make changes as needed.

Now you are ready to take the Unit Test and the Proficiency Assessment.

EXPRESS your ideas

Healthy Changes

In the lecture, you learned a "three-level approach" to encourage people to become healthier: better nutrition, more physical activity, and group support. Changing our habits and behaviors can be challenging. How can you inspire people to make healthier choices?

TASK Introduce a wellness program. Then deliver a short presentation to persuade the audience to join. Use nonverbal communication.

Prepare

1 Create a wellness program. Consider your audience. Think about the interests of your classmates. Using the three-level approach, brainstorm a list of "selling" points that will appeal to this particular audience. From your list, choose three points you can present with enthusiasm to inspire your audience to join your wellness program.

2 Organize the information from your notes into an outline. (Use the example outline to help you.) Do not write sentences on your outline. Use key words and phrases only.

3 Work with a partner. Tell your partner about how you plan to inspire the audience. Compare your outlines. Suggest changes to your outlines to make your presentations clearer or more inspiring.

Practice

4 Practice with your partner. What sections were convincing? Did you sound both enthusiastic and persuasive? How were your eye contact and gesturing? Use the *Unit 9 Presentation Evaluation Form* (in Appendix C) to give each other suggestions to improve your presentations.

5 Practice by yourself. Record your presentation or practice in front of a mirror. Pay attention to your body language and use clear gestures to show your enthusiasm. Use the Evaluation Form to evaluate your presentation.

Present

6 Deliver your presentation to the class. Try to speak enthusiastically and confidently.

7 When you finish, ask for audience questions: *Are there any questions? Are you ready to join my program?*

8 Listen to your classmates' presentations.

Evaluate

9 Use the Evaluation Form to evaluate your and your classmates' presentations. Be supportive: Give comments that will encourage your classmates to improve!

Presentation Strategy: Using nonverbal communication

A speaker's nonverbal communication is very important, especially if you are trying to inspire your listeners! Make your audience comfortable by smiling at them before you begin. Look at one listener while you speak to show your interest in that individual. (Look at one person for 3 full seconds!) Use vivid gestures and strong intonation. This will show your excitement and commitment. Your enthusiasm will influence your audience to try your idea.

TOPIC: HEALTHY CHANGES

Smile! Be enthusiastic!

Attention-getting opener

I Introduction: Main ideas

II Wellness through nutrition
  A Proposed change
  B 1st benefit
  C 2nd benefit

Transition to next main idea
III Wellness through activity
  A Proposed change
  B 1st benefit
  C 2nd benefit

Transition to next main idea
IV Wellness through group support
  A Proposed change
  B 1st benefit
  C 2nd benefit

Transition to conclusion
V Conclusion: Review of main ideas

10 21st Century Cities

CONNECT to the topic

More than half of the world's population now lives in cities. Cities all over the world are expanding rapidly. One question for the 21st century is: *What do we want life to be like in these cities?* A city is more than just a vast network of businesses, monuments, and buildings. It is a place people call home. How does the urban design of a city influence the people who live there?

A THINK ABOUT IT Consider these questions about urban living. Then compare responses with a partner.

- How important is it to you to live in a big city?
- What do you like about the city where you live now?
- What don't you like?
- What part of the city would you most like to live in? Why?

B TUNE IN Listen to a conversation between an urban designer and city councilman Allen Scheff. Then circle the best answers.

1 The designer and Councilman Scheff are meeting in order to **visit an art museum / enjoy the open space / walk through the plaza / plan an architecture project**.

2 The goals of the project are for the center to be a safe place to visit and to serve as **a business center / an attractive gathering spot / an education center**.

3 Councilman Scheff thinks **a plaza / old buildings / a lake / a monument** will make the city more attractive for everyone.

C PAIR WORK Work with a partner: Ask: *If you were a city planner, what would you like to change about your city?*

LEARNING OUTCOMES

In this unit you will:

- listen for expressions that signal connected ideas
- recognize main ideas from an urban planning lecture
- note details from an urban planning lecture
- identify and practice reduced and contracted words
- recognize and practice strategies for focusing on a topic
- review with a partner to prepare for the unit test
- give a presentation about improving your community, using persuasion

BUILD your vocabulary

A LISTEN The boldfaced words are from the unit lecture on urban planning. Listen to each sentence. Then choose the meaning of the boldfaced word.

1 The family had to **confront** some housing challenges when they moved to the city, but they eventually found a place to live.

    present   *face*   *provide*

2 The train system is **efficient.** It is at key locations throughout the city, is always on schedule, and uses little energy.

    expensive   *effective*   *wasteful*

3 Many large cities have a variety of **ethnic** groups who have come from all over the world.

    sincere   *cultural*   *routine*

4 The popular trend of shared resources, such as shared bicycles, is **expanding** rapidly in some cities.

    satisfying   *growing*   *protecting*

5 A **fundamental** challenge in all cities is providing adequate food for everyone.

    desirable   *dependable*   *basic*

6 To reduce traffic jams, the city plans to **initiate** a new traffic system next year.

    constrain   *start*   *fill*

7 The city decided to **institute** new guidelines for bicycles in order to reduce accidents.

    prevent   *establish*   *respond*

8 The city used video cameras to **monitor** who entered public buildings.

    reduce slightly   *coordinate*   *carefully watch*

9 Big cities worldwide are **projected** to keep growing rapidly.

    encouraged   *expected*   *discussed*

10 Mobility is important. People need to be able to get to work, school, and appointments **readily.**

    relatively   *enjoyably*   *quickly and easily*

B PAIR WORK Read the sentences in Column A and discuss the meanings of the boldfaced phrases. Then read sentences 1–5 aloud as your partner fills in the blanks in Column B. Switch roles for 6–10.

COLUMN A

1 More and more people are **living in** urban areas.

2 Many people **migrate from** rural areas to cities.

3 There are better **opportunities for** jobs.

4 Some people are **attracted to** cities for the excitement.

5 The family lived **on the outskirts of** the city, not in the city center.

6 Urban residents need to be **protected from** crime.

7 The police need to be **alerted to** dangerous situations.

8 People need to be able to **get around** the city easily.

9 Quality of life is **related to** people's mobility.

10 What are effective **approaches to** the challenges?

COLUMN B

1 More and more people are **living** _____ urban areas.

2 Many people **migrate** _____ rural areas to cities.

3 There are better **opportunities** _____ jobs.

4 Some people are **attracted** _____ cities for the excitement.

5 The family lived _____ **the outskirts** _____ the city, not in the city center.

6 Urban residents need to be **protected** _____ crime.

7 The police need to be **alerted** _____ dangerous situations.

8 People need to be able to **get** _____ the city easily.

9 Quality of life is **related** _____ people's mobility.

10 What are effective **approaches** _____ the challenges?

FOCUS your attention

Connected Ideas

Lecturers want you to understand how their ideas are connected. One way they do this is by pointing out a cause-and-effect relationship. Or a lecturer may try to help you make a connection to an idea mentioned earlier.

POINTING OUT CAUSE-AND-EFFECT RELATIONSHIPS	REFERRING TO AN EARLIER IDEA
If ... , then ...	*Do you recall ...*
Because (of) ...	*Think back to ...*
... This results in ...	*As I mentioned earlier ...*
... related to ...	

Another way a lecturer may show how ideas are connected is to give you supporting examples and sources.

GIVING SUPPORTING EXAMPLES AND SOURCES	
For example, ...	*According to ...*
Let's examine the case of ...	*One idea I'd like you to consider*

To take notes, you can show cause-and-effect relationships with an arrow (→) between ideas. Say you hear this: *The quality of farmland is getting worse, so people are pushed out.* Your notes might looks like this:

farmland worse → people pushed out

🔊 **A   TRY IT**   Listen to an excerpt from an urban planning lecture. What phrases do you hear that help you connect the ideas? Take notes.

B   PAIR WORK   Compare notes with a partner.

WATCH the lecture

Professor Helena Sonin

A **THINK ABOUT IT** You are about to watch the unit lecture on 21st century cities. What are some of the challenges that cities face as **people migrate to them?**

_____

_____

B **LISTEN FOR MAIN IDEAS** Close your book. Watch the lecture and take notes.

C **CHECK YOUR UNDERSTANDING** Use your notes. Answer the questions, based on the lecture. Circle *a*, *b*, or *c*.

1 What is the lecture mainly about?

  a transportation problems
  b the trend toward urban living
  c the opportunities in cities

2 In what order does the lecturer present the topics?

  a challenges of rapid growth, motivations for moving, effective solutions
  b challenges of rapid growth, effective solutions, motivations for moving
  c motivations for moving, challenges of rapid growth, effective solutions

3 Why does the speaker discuss push factors and pull factors? Choose TWO answers.

  a to describe urban life
  b to illustrate why people migrate
  c to show the situation is complex

4 What's the point of the speaker describing Daniel's experience?

  a to explain that cities are expanding
  b to describe the excitement of living in the city
  c to illustrate the types of problems many people face

5 What three challenges of people in cities are discussed?

  a jobs, food, housing
  b traffic, crime, entertainment
  c housing, transportation, safety

6 Which of the following statements would the lecturer agree with? Choose as many as appropriate.

  a Urban planners can't resolve these challenges.
  b There are big challenges, but creative solutions are possible.
  c The best solution is to prevent more migration.

D **LISTEN FOR DETAILS** Close your book. Watch the lecture again. Add details to your notes and correct any mistakes.

E **CHECK YOUR UNDERSTANDING** Use your notes. Choose the word or phrase that best completes each idea, based on the lecture.

1 A mega-city is defined as a city with a population over (**10 / 20**) million.

2 Limited job opportunities and poor farmland are examples of (**pull / push**) factors that (**send people away from / attract people to**) rural areas.

3 Better health care is an example of a (**pull / push**) factor that draws people to cities.

4 Daniel was attracted to the city by (**the excitement of city life / the opportunity to make money**).

5 According to the lecture, Daniel earned (**more / less**) money than he had in the country.

6 "People first" housing includes the idea that the housing is (**close to jobs / enjoyable to live in**).

7 The Intelligence Center approach is used to improve (**safety / transportation**).

8 The "healthy streets" program involves (**building sufficient housing / making the city more beautiful**).

9 The Brazilian light rail system reduced (**traffic / commuting times**) by (**15 / 50**) percent.

10 An "adaptive" traffic system means the traffic lights adjust to (**the time of day / the number of cars**).

HEAR the language

Reduced and Contracted Words

In natural speech, speakers sometimes **reduce** or **contract** function words such as prepositions, auxiliary verbs, pronouns, and conjunctions. By reducing these short words, the speaker keeps the rhythm of the sentence.

EXAMPLES	
One big challenge I **want to** discuss is ...	wanna
Today, I **want you** to think about ...	wancha
I'm guessing **most of** you have been to cities ...	mosta
There is no simple answer.	there's

A LISTEN Listen to the statements from the lecture. Circle the words that are reduced or contracted. The number of words is in parentheses.

1 (3) Today, we are going to consider three topics related to this trend.

2 (1) There are various "push factors" and various "pull factors."

3 (1) There are several factors that push people out of the countryside.

4 (1) Or perhaps there is religious or ethnic prejudice.

5 (2) Or, for health reasons, a family may choose to leave because a family member needs medical care.

6 (2) Daniel's goal was to get a job and send money back to his family.

7 (1) OK, he was pulled to the city by the opportunity to make money.

8 (2) As for a job, Daniel did manage to find one. But it required a one-hour bus ride each way.

9 (2) They want to assure that the new units are efficient, safe, and enjoyable to live in.

10 (2) Sydney, Australia, for example, has initiated an adaptive system of traffic flow.

B PAIR WORK   Work with a partner. Take turns saying the sentences. Pay attention to the reduced or contracted words.

TALK about the topic

Focusing on a Topic

A FOLLOW THE DISCUSSION Watch as the students talk about the lecture. Read each comment. Then check (√) the student who makes the comment.

Hugh Shelley Ben Kenzie

	Hugh	Shelley	Ben	Kenzie
1 "I hadn't considered all these reasons. The pushes and the pulls."	☐	☐	☐	☐
2 "I'd only thought of the pulls, like better job opportunities."	☐	☐	☐	☐
3 "I never really thought about how cities really go through the same problems."	☐	☐	☐	☐
4 "What does 'the inverse of push factors' mean?"	☐	☐	☐	☐

B LEARN THE STRATEGIES Watch the discussion again. Listen closely for the comments. Then check (√) the discussion strategy the student uses. More than one answer may be correct.

	Asking for clarification or confirmation	Expressing an opinion	Focusing on a topic
1 Ben: "That stuff. The reasons are interesting."	☐	☐	☐
2 Shelley: "Before that, I want to go back to the reasons for migration."	☐	☐	☐
3 Hugh: "You were saying all cities face similar challenges. ... Can you expand on that?"	☐	☐	☐
4 Hugh: "Yeah, those are big challenges for cities."	☐	☐	☐
5 Shelley: "You know, that's just not realistic."	☐	☐	☐

Discussion Strategy When you **focus on a topic**, you show that you want to concentrate the discussion on a specific point or idea. A common way to focus on a topic is to state your intention: *I want to focus on ... , I'd like to start off with talking about ... , I'd like to go back to the topic of ...* . Here are common ways to ask someone to focus on an idea or topic: *The lecturer said [cities are overcrowded]. Can anyone expand on that?* or *The lecturer talked about [push factors and pull factors]. Can anyone explain that to me?*

C TRY IT In a small group, discuss one or more of these topics. Try to use the discussion strategies you have learned.

- Kenzie says, "Maybe people should stop migrating there." Is this a realistic solution to the challenges cities are confronting? Give reasons.
- What are specific things that can be done to make cities more livable and enjoyable for different age groups?
- What changes would you like to see in a city in your country in ten years?

REVIEW your notes

REVIEW Read over your notes. Do you have clear notes on the three topics of the lecture? Do your notes include examples and details? Work with a partner to retell the main ideas of the lecture in your own words. Then complete these notes. Add details and examples.

Topic 1: factors that motivate people to move to cities

    Push factors:

    Pull factors:

    Example: Daniel, Lima, Peru

    Reasons he migrated:

    Challenges he confronted:

Topic 2: fundamental challenges of cities growing rapidly

    1

    2

    3

Topic 3: possible solutions to each challenge

    1

    2

    3

TIP!

Remember: Focus on the relationships between the ideas you hear.

🔊 **Now you are ready to take the Unit Test and the Proficiency Assessment.**

EXPRESS your ideas

A Great Place to Live

This unit lecture explored ways of improving cities. Now think of a city you know well, such as your hometown or the city you live in now. How can it be improved?

TASK Observe two problems in your community. Find solutions. Then give a short presentation on your plan. Try to persuade your audience.

Prepare

1 See your community through the eyes of an urban planner. Brainstorm the important issues the city where you live may have. (For example, public transportation services, parking, traffic signals, access to shopping or good housing, personal safety, etc.) Choose two issues. Consider one possible solution for each issue. Identify the benefits of your proposed solution.

2 Organize your ideas into an outline. (Use the example outline to help you.) Use your list of problems as your main ideas. Your description of the problems, your solutions, and the benefits of your solutions are your supporting details.

3 Create a visual presentation using images to illustrate the problems. Use short *phrases* to support your main ideas and details. Start each phrase on one slide with the same part of speech. (For example, all bullet points on one slide begin with a verb.)

4 Work with a partner. Share information about your city's issues and your proposed solutions. Compare your outlines. Look at your slides. Make changes to your outline and slides as needed.

Practice

5 Practice with your partner. Take turns giving your presentations. Practice showing your visuals. Do your images clearly show the problems? Does each slide use short phrases starting with the same part of speech? Use the *Unit 10 Presentation Evaluation Form* (in Appendix C) to give each other suggestions to improve your presentations.

Present

6 Deliver your presentation to the class. Remember to glance at your outline occasionally and then look at your audience as you speak. Don't read from your slides. Try to speak enthusiastically and confidently. Briefly review the benefits of your proposed changes in your conclusion.

7 When you finish, ask for audience questions: *Are there any questions? Are you convinced we need to make these changes?*

8 Listen to your classmates' presentations.

Evaluate

9 Use the Evaluation Form to evaluate your and your classmates' presentations.

Presentation Strategy: Persuading your audience

For some presentations, you will need to persuade your audience to accept your opinion or plan. To convince your audience, first describe the problems that you see. Provide visual evidence. Then present your plan for addressing these problems. Finally, explain the benefits your plan will bring to your audience. Use details to support your ideas.

TOPIC: A GREAT PLACE TO LIVE

Attention-getting opener

I Introduction: Main ideas (issues, plan to resolve issues, and benefits)

Transition to challenge #1
II Issue #1 *Slide*
  A Description of problem
  B Solution *Slide*
    1 Benefit #1
    2 Benefit #2

Transition to challenge #2
III Issue #2 *Slide*
  A Description of problem
  B Solution *Slide*
    1 Benefit #1
    2 Benefit #2

Transition to conclusion
IV Conclusion
  A Review of main ideas
  B Question about audience agreement and support

11 DNA Testing

CONNECT to the topic

We each have our own set of DNA—our genome—that makes each of us unique. It contains genetic information from our parents that determines our appearance and talents, and even what diseases we may be at risk of developing. Scientists can now identify an organism by testing its DNA. This discovery has sparked an explosion of possibilities in the field of biotechnology.

A THINK ABOUT IT Take this survey about traits. Then compare responses with a partner. **How are you similar to family members? Different?**

	You	Mother	Father	Sister or Brother
• eye color				
• hair color				
• height				
• personality				
• talents				
• interests				

B TUNE IN Listen to a conversation between genetics counselor Dr. Navdeep Shan and a patient. Then work with a partner to answer the questions, based on the conversation.

1 Why does the patient want to take the test?

_____

2 What does Dr. Shan mean by "predictive testing"?

_____

3 Why will Dr. Shan need blood samples from both the patient and his father?

_____

C PAIR WORK Work with a partner. Ask: *What other traits do you share with your family members—father, mother, brothers, sisters, aunts, uncles, cousins, and grandparents? Which of these traits are inherited (you were born with them) and which of these traits are learned (you acquired them as you grew up)?*

LEARNING OUTCOMES
In this unit you will:
- practice using a graphic organizer to link information
- recognize central ideas from a biology lecture
- fact-check statements from a biology lecture
- identify and practice stressing words to make ideas clear
- recognize and practice strategies for getting a discussion started
- organize and add to your lecture notes to prepare for the unit test
- give a presentation about a scientific breakthrough, using quotations

BUILD your vocabulary

A LISTEN The boldfaced words are from the unit lecture on DNA testing. Listen to each sentence. Then guess the meaning of the boldfaced word.

1 The police wanted **access to** DNA samples taken from the suspect. But the judge refused to release the samples.

2 The researchers **concentrated on** the role genetics play in our health. They didn't focus on anything else.

3 Dr. Hassan couldn't figure out what was wrong with her patient. She decided to use genetic testing to help **diagnose** the patient's disease.

4 In the crime lab, scientists **extract** DNA from samples of hair, skin, and fingernails. After they remove the DNA from the samples, they test it.

5 The twin brothers looked a lot alike, but they weren't **identical** twins; one had brown hair and one had blond hair.

6 The lab technician saw that the two blood samples didn't **match**, so she concluded that the blood was from two different people.

7 The **medical** field uses DNA tests to find out who is at risk for certain diseases.

8 The Morettis wanted to have a baby, so they had a DNA test. It **revealed** that their baby might inherit a genetic disorder from the father.

9 **Statistically**, it's very unlikely that two people will have the same DNA profile. The chance of this happening is less than 1 percent.

10 Our DNA contains genetic information such as eye color and other **traits** passed down from a mother and father to their child.

B TRY IT Complete each sentence with the correct word or phrase.

extract	matched	medical	reveal	statistically

1 DNA research has had a big impact on the _____ field, particularly on how doctors work with their patients.

2 The lab results showed that the hair found in the suspect's car _____ the hair of the victim's cat.

3 DNA testing may _____ that something isn't normal in a person's genes. For example, it may show a person is at risk for a disease.

4 It's unlikely _____ for two DNA fingerprints to be the same.

5 To create a DNA fingerprint, scientists _____ DNA from samples taken from various parts of the body.

access to	concentrated on	diagnose	identical	trait

6 It took doctors a year to _____ the baby's disease.

7 Height is just one _____ children inherit from parents.

8 The lab workers _____ identifying the murder victim.

9 These two fingerprints aren't _____ ; they're different.

10 The company had _____ employees' personal information.

C **PAIR WORK** Work with a partner. Read the sentences in Column A and discuss the meanings of the boldfaced phrases. Then read sentences 1–5 aloud as your partner fills in the blanks in Column B. Switch roles for 6–10.

COLUMN A

1 The evidence **at the crime scene** was a strand of hair.

2 Everyone has a **combination of** genetic traits from their parents.

3 Two sisters may **end up with** the same eye color.

4 There was a **match between** the two DNA samples.

5 A probe is a tool **used by** scientists in DNA testing.

6 The test showed that the woman was **at risk for** Alzheimer's disease.

7 With DNA testing comes **concerns about** privacy.

8 Doctors give DNA tests **for one of two reasons**.

9 Some diseases are **linked to** our genes.

10 What are the **pros and cons of** DNA testing?

COLUMN B

1 The evidence _____ **the crime scene** was a strand of hair.

2 Everyone has a **combination** _____ genetic traits from their parents.

3 Two sisters may **end** _____ _____ the same eye color.

4 There was a **match** _____ the two DNA samples.

5 A probe is a tool **used** _____ scientists in DNA testing.

6 The test showed that the woman was _____ **risk** _____ Alzheimer's disease.

7 With DNA testing comes **concerns** _____ privacy.

8 Doctors give DNA tests _____ **one** _____ **two reasons**.

9 Some diseases are **linked** _____ our genes.

10 What are the **pros** _____ **cons** _____ DNA testing?

FOCUS your attention

Graphic Organizers

Sometimes, a lecturer presents a lot of technical information or details—for example, in describing a process. A graphic organizer is one way to help you link and remember information. You can fill in information as you listen and then add more later when you review your notes.

A speaker often uses the following signal words when describing a process. When you hear these words, move on to the next part of your organizer, as shown below.

DESCRIBING A PROCESS	
They start by ... / First ...	After that ...
Next ...	And then ... / At that point ...
Then ...	Finally ...

Your notes might look like this:

They start by / First ...	→	Next ...	→	Then ...

↓

Finally ...	←	And then ... / At that point	←	After that ...

A TRY IT Listen to an excerpt from a crime investigation seminar. What words and phrases do you hear that signal the process? Take notes.

B PAIR WORK Compare notes with a partner.

WATCH the lecture

Professor Robert Myers

A THINK ABOUT IT You are about to watch the unit lecture on some uses of DNA testing. What uses do you know of? Write your ideas.

_____

_____

B LISTEN FOR MAIN IDEAS Close your book. Watch the lecture and take notes.

C CHECK YOUR UNDERSTANDING Use your notes. Answer the questions, based on the lecture. Circle *a*, *b*, or *c*.

1 What is the lecture mainly about?

   a how doctors use DNA testing to cure diseases
   b how to create a DNA fingerprint and some uses
   c types of genetic disorders that cause diseases

2 In what order does the speaker present the topics?

   a medical uses, privacy concerns, creating a DNA fingerprint
   b creating a DNA fingerprint, privacy concerns, medical uses
   c creating a DNA fingerprint, medical uses, privacy concerns

3 What is DNA fingerprinting? Choose TWO answers.

   a making a copy of a person's DNA
   b creating a set of data about someone using DNA
   c creating an "ID" of someone using DNA samples from different parts of the body

4 What's one way a crime lab can use DNA testing?

   a to identify a car accident victim
   b to look for DNA matches between a suspect and evidence from a crime scene
   c to let the police know there was a crime

5 What is the connection between genetic disorders and disease?

   a Genetic disorders increase the risk of getting a disease.
   b Scientists know genetic disorders always cause diseases.
   c Scientists don't know if there's a link between genetic disorders and diseases.

6 What is the speaker's general attitude toward DNA testing?

   a DNA testing is very beneficial.
   b There are privacy issues we need to consider.
   c DNA testing should be done more often.

D **LISTEN FOR DETAILS** Close your book. Watch the lecture again. Add details to your notes and correct any mistakes.

E **CHECK YOUR UNDERSTANDING** Decide if the statements are *T* (true) or *F* (false), based on the lecture. Correct any false statements.

_____ **1** Another way to say "DNA fingerprint" is "DNA profile."

_____ **2** The speaker thinks it's statistically likely that a brother and sister will have identical genetic information.

_____ **3** DNA testing proved that Marie Antoinette's son escaped from prison.

_____ **4** A crime lab uses probes to see if DNA samples from a suspect match DNA samples from evidence at a crime scene.

_____ **5** The more probes that match, the stronger the case against the suspect.

_____ **6** Scientists have found that DNA identification in a crime lab is 100 percent foolproof.

_____ **7** According to the speaker, there are more than 16,000 genetic disorders.

_____ **8** The speaker says that a mutation—a change in a gene—will definitely cause a disease.

_____ **9** The speaker says that one benefit of DNA testing is that it might save someone's life.

_____ **10** The speaker is concerned about who should have access to someone's DNA profile.

HEAR the language

Stressing Words to Make Ideas Clear

Speakers help listeners understand their ideas by putting extra **stress** on particular words. To create word stress, the speaker uses a slightly slower rate of speech, a higher pitch, and an increased volume on the most important word in each thought group.

> **EXAMPLES**
>
> *So, / each of us has our <u>own</u> DNA, / our own <u>combination</u> of genetic information / from our <u>parents</u>. /*
> *However, / <u>other</u> genetic information / received from the parents will be <u>different</u>, / which is why they*
> *<u>look</u> different. /*

A LISTEN Listen to the statements and questions from the lecture. Underline the word that receives the most emphasis in each thought group.

1 Keep in mind that DNA is in every cell in the body, / and that all of these cells / contain the same genetic information. /

2 They use the data / to create / the DNA fingerprint. /

3 Statistically, / it is very unlikely / that any two people / will have identical fingerprints. /

4 In the crime lab, / scientists use DNA samples from the suspect / and DNA samples from the evidence / at the crime scene. /

5 When the probes are put in with the DNA samples from the suspect / and the DNA samples from the evidence, / the probes show / if the two sets of samples match. /

6 For example, / suppose the only evidence / at the crime scene / is blood / from the suspect. /

7 They design four probes, / one for each sample, / and they get four matches—bingo! /

8 And a DNA test can show / if someone has a mutation in a gene / that puts them at risk / for the disease. /

9 For example, / it now appears that the disease Alzheimer's, / which damages memory in older people / is linked to our genes. /

10 Would you want people, / especially people you don't know, / to have access / to your DNA fingerprint? /

B PAIR WORK Work with a partner. Take turns saying the sentences. Pay attention to your word stress in each thought group.

TALK about the topic

Getting a Discussion Started

A FOLLOW THE DISCUSSION Watch as the students talk about DNA testing. Read each opinion. Then check (√) who agrees with it.

Hannah   River   Manny   Mia

	Hannah	River	Manny	Mia
1 Doctors and the government already have all other personal information.	☐	☐	☐	☐
2 If I have a DNA test, it's nobody's business but my own.	☐	☐	☐	☐
3 DNA is good information for the police to have access to, like in the example of crime.	☐	☐	☐	☐
4 DNA results that show risk for disease just cause worry.	☐	☐	☐	☐

B LEARN THE STRATEGIES Watch the discussion again. Listen closely for the comments. Then check (√) the discussion strategy the student uses. More than one answer may be correct.

	Disagreeing	Expressing an opinion	Getting a discussion started
1 River: "Yeah, isn't she great?"	☐	☐	☐
2 Hannah: "Sorry, guys … That's not really why we're here. We're supposed to … "	☐	☐	☐
3 River: "Well, in my opinion, I mean, it doesn't really matter."	☐	☐	☐
4 Manny: "Come on. That's not true."	☐	☐	☐
5 Mia: "I think we're all going to worry about something."	☐	☐	☐

Discussion Strategy   Everyone's time is valuable, so it's important to **start an organized discussion** on time. You may need to politely interrupt chitchat. Expressions for getting started include: *Sorry. But we need to get started. Is everyone ready? River, would you like to start?*

C TRY IT In a small group, discuss one or more of these topics. Try to use the discussion strategies you have learned.

- Do you agree that the results of your DNA test are nobody else's business?
- In what situations might it be good for others to have access to your DNA information?
- Have you heard of people being freed from prison because of DNA testing? If so, what were the details?

REVIEW your notes

REVIEW Use your notes. Work with a partner to complete the organizer and answer the questions below. Then retell the main ideas of the lecture in your own words.

Process for creating a DNA fingerprint

| First, scientists take samples from different parts of the body such as blood. | → | Next, they extract _____ from the cells in the samples. | → | Then they use a _____ to read _____. |

Process in a crime lab for comparing DNA from a suspect with DNA from evidence

| Scientists take DNA samples from _____. | → | They also take DNA samples from _____. |

↓

| Finally, the more matches they have, the more _____. | ← | After that, they design _____ to see if _____. |

TIP!

Each square in your graphic organizer should contain the key information about a step in the process.

- What two medical uses of DNA testing are mentioned?
- What is the relationship between genetic disorders and diseases?
- What are the pros and cons of DNA testing in medicine?
- What privacy questions does the speaker consider?

🔊 **Now you are ready to take the Unit Test and the Proficiency Assessment.**

EXPRESS your ideas

A Scientific Advance

The lecturer in this unit discussed scientific advances in DNA testing. Every year, there are new advances in science. Which areas of science interest you?

TASK **With a partner, choose a recent advance in science. Then give a short presentation about it. Include your own opinions and at least two quotations from credible sources about the impact of this recent advance.**

Prepare

1 With your partner, choose an area of research, such as one the following:

> DNA research: Archeology studies of past civilizations or finding one's own family tree
>
> Energy: Generating clean energy
>
> Medicine: Diagnosing and treating diseases
>
> Climate science: Addressing global warming
>
> Robotics: Designing human companions

Do online research. Find quotations from credible sources about this advance. Take careful notes. Write down the exact words in the quote. Do not paraphrase the ideas.

2 With your partner, organize your research into an outline. (Use the example outline to help you.) For Main Idea 1, describe the advance. For Main Idea 2, describe how it benefits us. Use key words and phrases to add details. Add transitions. Include quotations from credible sources on the impact of this advance in science.

3 Discuss your outlines. Talk about your findings. Make changes as needed.

Practice

4 Practice with your partner. Establish roles so that you are comfortable presenting with a partner. As you move between speakers, be sure to include effective transitions. Use the *Unit 11 Presentation Evaluation Form* (in Appendix C) to give each other suggestions to improve your presentation.

5 Practice with another pair. Take turns giving your presentations. Did you say "quote" and "end of quote" to start and end your quotations? Did you move smoothly between speakers?

Present

6 Deliver your presentation to the class. Use your outline. Remember to glance at your outline occasionally and then look at your audience as you speak.

7 When you finish, ask for audience questions: *Are there any questions? Do you have any other ideas about how this discovery will help us today?*

Evaluate

8 Use the Evaluation Form to evaluate your and your classmates' presentations. Be supportive: Give comments that will encourage your classmates to improve!

Presentation Strategy: Using quotations

You can strengthen your presentations by incorporating quotations from credible sources. In schools and universities in the US and in many other countries, students are required to indicate when they use someone else's ideas, or when they say another person's exact words. You can start your quotation with one of these introductory phrases:

As John Smith said, quote, " … ." End quote.

In John Smith's words, " … ."

John Smith has stated " … ."

To quote John Smith, " … ."

TOPIC: A SCIENTIFIC ADVANCE

I Introduction: Major scientific advance

Transition to main idea #1
II Main idea #1: What it is
  A Supporting detail: Description of the advance
  B Supporting detail: Quotation from research

Transition to main idea #2
III Main idea #2: How this advance will help us
  A Supporting detail: Examples of what will happen now
  B Supporting detail: Quotation from research

Transition to conclusion
IV Conclusion
  A Restatement of main idea
  B Questions from the group

12 Risk Management

CONNECT to the topic

We know we can't control nature. We know every year there are natural hazards such as tornados, hurricanes, earthquakes, floods, and wildfires. We also know that we can *prepare* for them so that they don't automatically become natural disasters.

A THINK ABOUT IT Consider these questions about natural disasters. Then compare responses with a partner.

- What natural disasters have you heard about recently?
- Have you experienced a tornado, hurricane, earthquake, or flood? If so, what happened?
- What seem to be the biggest problems for people right after a natural disaster?

B TUNE IN Listen to a journalist's interview with Tanya Green, a resident of New Orleans. Then work with a partner to answer the questions, based on the conversation.

1 What event are they discussing?

_____

2 Why didn't Tanya Green's family leave their house right away?

_____

3 How long was Green's family on the roof before they were rescued?

_____

4 What does "a silver lining" mean? What was the silver lining in this story?

_____

C PAIR WORK Work with a partner. Ask: *If you had to leave your home because of a natural disaster, what would you take with you? Why? How would you use social media to reconnect with family, friends, and emergency services?*

LEARNING OBJECTIVES
In this unit you will:
- practice marking your notes for questions and follow-up
- articulate the key ideas of a public administration lecture
- extract details from a public administration lecture
- identify and practice pausing after thought groups
- recognize and practice strategies for asking for opinions and ideas
- discuss the lecture with a partner to prepare for the unit test
- give a presentation about a survivor's story and answer audience questions

BUILD your vocabulary

A LISTEN The boldfaced words are from the unit lecture on emergency planning.
Listen to each sentence. Then match the meaning to the boldfaced word.

_____ **1** The government will **allocate** part of its budget for roads, but it also needs to budget money for schools.

_____ **2** After a natural disaster, people should **cooperate** by doing what the officials ask.

_____ **3** It's important to **minimize** the impact of hurricanes. We can reduce the damage by being prepared.

    a do what someone is asked to do
    b make the amount of something as small as possible
    c decide to allow a certain amount of money to be used

_____ **4** Sometimes, people **ignore** government orders to evacuate. They don't listen to instructions to leave, even though it might be dangerous to stay home.

_____ **5** Experts can't **predict** exactly when an earthquake will occur.

_____ **6** Governments set spending **priorities**. What's needed more: better health care or more public transportation?

_____ **7** The Gulf Coast region of the United States is disaster-**prone**; in other words, a disaster is more likely to occur there than in some other parts of the country.

    d likely to do something or to suffer from something
    e say that something will happen before it happens
    f the things that are most important and need attention first
    g refuse to pay attention to

_____ **8** Our local public safety officer held an informational meeting about what to do during a tornado, in hopes of **mitigating** the townspeople's fears.

_____ **9** Educational programs **targeted** at students help them understand the risks of local natural hazards.

_____ **10** It's difficult for every citizen to be totally prepared for a natural disaster. **Ultimately**, it's up to the government to try its best to keep people safe.

_____ **11** The hurricane caused **widespread** damage: Houses were destroyed throughout the region.

    h in the end
    i happening in many places or situations or with many people
    j aimed at, developed for
    k making less severe, not as bad

B **PAIR WORK** Work with a partner. Read the sentences in Column A and discuss the meanings of the boldfaced phrases. Then read sentences 1–4 aloud as your partner fills in the blanks in Column B. Switch roles for 5–8.

COLUMN A

1 Small earthquakes usually don't cause damage. **By the same token**, there are always exceptions.

2 Fortunately, the hurricane **died out** and caused no problems.

3 Let's look at some factors **involved in** generating an emergency plan.

4 Experts can't **predict with 100 percent accuracy**. They don't know for sure when a storm will hit.

5 Preparedness is **the state of being ready**.

6 The government needs to establish a **channel of communication** with scientists.

7 The government had a strong emergency plan **in place** in many cities. They were well prepared.

8 **The logic behind** the UNESCO program is that educating children will benefit everyone.

COLUMN B

1 Small earthquakes usually don't cause damage. _____ **the same token**, there are always exceptions.

2 Fortunately, the hurricane **died** _____ and caused no problems.

3 Let's look at some factors **involved** _____ generating an emergency plan.

4 Experts can't **predict** _____ **100 percent accuracy**. They don't know for sure when a storm will hit.

5 Preparedness is **the state** _____ **being ready**.

6 The government needs to establish a **channel** _____ **communication** with scientists.

7 The government had a strong emergency plan _____ **place** in many cities. They were well prepared.

8 **The logic** _____ the UNESCO program is that educating children will benefit everyone.

FOCUS your attention

Questions

As you listen to a lecture, you may not quite understand what the speaker says, or you may simply want to know more. You can write a question mark (?) in the margin of your notes to help you keep track of the questions you have. Sometimes, you're lucky and the speaker answers your question later on in the lecture. But other times you'll need to find the answer yourself after class.

Say the speaker mentions Hurricane Katrina, but you miss the year it happened. Later, the speaker says, *As I mentioned, Hurricane Katrina was in 2005.* You can quickly write down the date, draw an arrow up, and continue taking notes. Then, when you review your notes, you can make revisions. Your notes might look like this:

> ? Hurricane Katrina: 20_____
>
> Aug. 23 — started near Bahamas
>
>   affected: north-central Gulf Coast
>
>   • 1 of the 5 most deadly hurricanes in US history
>
>   • 6th strongest Atlantic hurricane
>
>   • 3rd strongest to make landfall in US
>
> EX: New Orleans, LA
>
>   levees: walls to hold back water
>
>   • broke • design/construction issues
>
>   evacuation ordered Aug. 28 ~ 26,000 stayed
>
> IMPACT: total deaths: 1,836 + missing: 705
>
> 2005

A TRY IT **Listen to an excerpt from a conference on emergency planning. Take notes. Write a question mark (?) in your notes if you miss information. Use arrows if you hear it later or get it from another student.**

B PAIR WORK **What questions do you have? Compare notes with a partner.**

WATCH the lecture

A THINK ABOUT IT You are about to watch the unit lecture on emergency planning. What are important considerations for a government? Rank this list from 1 to 6 (1 = most important).

_____ buy food, blankets, emergency supplies

_____ train emergency workers

_____ tell the public what the emergency plan is

_____ have temporary housing ready

_____ give emergency cell phones to every household

_____ build emergency animal shelters for pets

Professor David Reed

B LISTEN FOR MAIN IDEAS Close your book. Watch the lecture and take notes.

C CHECK YOUR UNDERSTANDING Use your notes. Answer the questions, based on the lecture. Circle *a*, *b*, or *c*.

1 Why does the speaker compare natural hazards and natural disasters?

   a to emphasize the different types of natural disasters
   b to emphasize that they are not the same thing
   c to emphasize that they can happen anywhere

2 What is the main point of the lecture?

   a that it's possible to prevent some natural disasters
   b that emergency plans are vital
   c both *a* and *b*

3 What is a government's first step in developing an emergency plan?

   a setting spending priorities
   b evaluating services
   c identifying the natural hazards it faces

4 What is one of the biggest challenges for governments and scientists?

   a organizing emergency supplies
   b knowing what to tell the public and when
   c trying to control natural hazards

5 What is the speaker's main point about Hurricane Katrina and the public?

   a Many services are needed.
   b Information isn't useful if it's ignored.
   c It hit New Orleans.

6 What seems to be the speaker's attitude toward the UNESCO program?

   a It shouldn't be a spending priority.
   b It's a very positive step.
   c It's not an essential part of emergency preparation.

D LISTEN FOR DETAILS Close your book. Watch the lecture again. Add details to your notes and correct any mistakes.

E CHECK YOUR UNDERSTANDING Use your notes. Decide if the statements are *T* (true) or *F* (false), based on the lecture. Correct any false statements.

_____ **1** A natural hazard means there is the potential for a lot of damage.

_____ **2** The speaker mentions the earthquake in Pakistan in 2005 as an example of a terrible disaster.

_____ **3** Disaster mitigation means preparing for a natural disaster so that people will suffer less.

_____ **4** The speaker mentions earthquakes and typhoons as examples of natural hazards in the United States.

_____ **5** If scientists predict incorrectly, the public may not be willing to cooperate in the future.

_____ **6** Sixty-one percent of the people in New Orleans didn't evacuate because they didn't want to leave.

_____ **7** The fourth factor in an emergency plan includes determining if there are enough trained emergency workers.

_____ **8** Setting spending priorities is difficult because governments know natural disasters always happen.

_____ **9** The main goal of the UNESCO program is to make just children safer.

_____ **10** The speaker mentions Turkey, Japan, and Cuba as countries where UNESCO safety programs have been successful.

HEAR the language

Key Words in Thought Groups

Speakers always make a brief **pause** after each thought group. When you hear a pause, you have a moment to focus on the **key words** you've just heard. And you can prepare for new information to follow.

> **EXAMPLE**
> *The **topic** of today's class / is **reducing risks** / from **natural hazards** /*

A LISTEN Listen to the statements and questions from the lecture. Use a slash (/) to mark the speaker's pauses in each sentence. Listen again and circle the most important word(s) in each thought group. Note that punctuation indicating a pause has been removed.

1 Notice I said natural hazards not natural disasters

2 Three prime examples of this are the earthquake in Pakistan in 2005 Hurricane Katrina in the US in the same year and the tsunami in the Indian Ocean in 2004

3 To *mitigate* means to make less severe not as bad

4 The problem is experts can't predict natural hazards with 100 percent accuracy

5 Despite this public officials still have to decide what to tell the public and when

6 But if they tell people to evacuate and then nothing happens people may get angry

7 We know some stayed because they had no transportation no choice

8 Is there a way to inform the public about the emergency plan so they know where to go and what to do before during and after a natural disaster

9 Well related to this evaluation is the fifth and final factor setting spending priorities

10 Experts agree that educating the public especially children about the risks is essential

B PAIR WORK Work with a partner. Take turns saying the sentences. Remember to make pauses after each thought group. And be sure to emphasize the key words.

TALK about the topic

Asking for Opinions or Ideas

A FOLLOW THE DISCUSSION Watch as the students talk about natural disasters. Read each idea. Then check (√) who agrees with it. More than one student may agree.

Alana   Rob   Molly   Ayman

	Alana	Rob	Molly	Ayman
1 Nature can be dangerous, but it's not always destructive.	☐	☐	☐	☐
2 People have a responsibility to stay safe.	☐	☐	☐	☐
3 Money is probably a big reason that hazards become disasters.	☐	☐	☐	☐
4 Safety education is priceless.	☐	☐	☐	☐

B LEARN THE STRATEGIES Watch the discussion again. Listen closely for the comments. Then check (√) the discussion strategy or strategies the student uses. More than one answer may be correct.

	Agreeing	Asking for opinions or ideas	Offering a fact or example
1 **Ayman:** "So, what did you guys think of the lecture?"	☐	☐	☐
2 **Molly:** "Yeah, not only that, but it also … "	☐	☐	☐
3 **Molly:** "Like with Hurricane Katrina in the US back in 2005?"	☐	☐	☐
4 **Ayman:** "Like, look at earthquakes—how can someone be responsible for something so unexpected?"	☐	☐	☐
5 **Molly:** "I think education, like the UNESCO program, is one inexpensive way to make a really big difference."	☐	☐	☐

Discussion Strategy Who doesn't appreciate being asked about their thoughts on a subject? By **asking for opinions and ideas**, you'll not only help others become involved in the discussion, but also enrich the discussion itself as a result. It's as easy as asking, *What do you think?* The next step—listening—is where your learning begins!

C TRY IT In a small group, discuss one or more of these topics. Try to use the discussion strategies you have learned.

- How can city officials get citizens involved in emergency preparedness?
- Do you think an emergency response plan should be a spending priority?
- Do you think people should rely on the government or on each other during national emergencies?

REVIEW your notes

REVIEW **REVIEW** Work with a partner. Use your notes. If you have any question marks (?) in your notes, see if your partner can help you with the answers. You can ask yourself or your partner questions using the following phrases. Then complete the notes below.

I wonder why …	*I wonder what caused …*
I'd like to know …	*I wonder why (the speaker) concluded that …*
What does … mean?	

I. *Natural hazard vs. natural disaster:*

II. *Emergency Response Plan*

    Factor 1:

    Factor 2:

    Factor 3:

    Factor 4:

    Factor 5:

III. *UNESCO program*

    A. Goals:

    B. Ex.'s of programs in countries:

TIP!

Mark places in your notes where you missed information or didn't understand something. This will remind you to follow up later.

🔊 **Now you are ready to take the Unit Test and the Proficiency Assessment.**

EXPRESS your ideas

A Survivor's Story

In the lecture, the professor discussed natural hazards and important factors in planning for them. What strategies do you think will prepare you best to handle a natural disaster?

TASK **Learn about someone's survival story. Then give a short presentation about it and what it has taught you about preparedness. Address audience questions.**

Prepare

1 Interview a person you know who has survived a natural disaster or go online to learn about a survivor's story. Use a search term such as "stories of people who survived natural disasters" to learn about people like Zahrul Fuadi, who survived two tsunamis, or Daryl Jane, who survived for 14 days in a snowstorm.

2 Organize your research into an outline. (Use the example outline to help you.) Include a disaster timeline and the survival strategies the person used. Then add what you learned from how this person handled the challenges.

3 Work with a partner. Compare your outlines. Ask each other questions. Make changes to your outline as needed.

Practice

4 Practice with your partner. Did you rephrase your partner's questions? Use the *Presentation Evaluation Form* (in Appendix C) to give each other suggestions.

5 Practice by yourself. Make sure you present survivor's story clearly, and are also clear about how you plan to apply to your own life what you learned from this person's experience.

Present

6 Deliver your presentation to the class. Use your outline. Remember not to read from it.

7 When you finish, ask for audience questions: *Do you have any questions about this story?* Be sure to rephrase each question you are asked before giving an answer.

Evaluate

8 Use the Evaluation Form to evaluate your and your classmates' presentations.

Presentation Strategy: Answering audience questions

Answering questions after your presentation is often very challenging because you can't always know what audience members will ask. Before you begin your answer, repeat or rephrase the question to make sure all your audience heard it. Rephrasing a question also gives you time to organize your response. Here are some ways you can rephrase a question:

Your question is ...

I think you are asking ...

So you want to know ...

You're asking ...

TOPIC: A SURVIVOR'S STORY

I Introduction: Main ideas

Transition to main idea #1 (Survivor's story)
II Main idea #1: Background information
   A Supporting detail: Where disaster happened
   B Supporting detail: When disaster happened

Transition
III Main idea #2: Survivor
   A Supporting detail: Description of survivor (age, nationality, etc.)
   B Supporting detail: Background information about survivor (profession, experience, etc.)

Transition
IV Main idea #3: Disaster timeline
   A Supporting detail: 1st important event
   B Supporting detail: 2nd important event

Transition
V Main idea #4: Survival strategies
   A Supporting detail: Survivor's 1st strategy
   B Supporting detail: Survivor's 2nd strategy

Transition
VI Main idea #5: What I learned for my own life
   A Supporting detail: 1st key idea
   B Supporting detail: 2nd key idea

Transition
VII Conclusion
   A Restatement of main ideas
   B Questions and answers

APPENDIX A

Academic Word List

Numbers indicate the sublist of the Academic Word List. For example, *abandon* and its family members are in Sublist 8. Sublist 1 contains the most frequent words in the list, and Sublist 10 contains the least frequent. **Boldfacing** indicates that the word is taught in *Contemporary Topics 2*. The page number of the section where the word is taught is indicated in parentheses.

abandon	8	anticipate	9	bulk	9	compile	10
abstract	6	apparent	4	capable	6	complement	8
academy	5	append	8	capacity	5	**complex** (p. 33)	2
access (p. 103)	4	**appreciate** (p. 63)	8	category	2	component	3
accommodate	9	approach	1	cease	9	compound	5
accompany	8	appropriate	2	challenge	5	comprehensive	7
accumulate	8	**approximate** (p. 83)	4	channel	7	comprise	7
accurate (p. 43)	6	arbitrary	8	chapter	2	compute	2
achieve	2	area	1	chart	8	conceive	10
acknowledge (p. 13)	6	aspect	2	chemical	7	**concentrate** (p. 103)	4
acquire (p. 33)	2	assemble	10	circumstance	3	concept	1
adapt	7	**assess** (p. 43)	1	cite	6	conclude	2
adequate	4	**assign** (p. 3)	6	civil	4	concurrent	9
adjacent	10	assist	2	clarify	8	conduct	2
adjust	5	assume	1	**classic** (p. 3)	7	confer	4
administrate	2	assure	9	clause	5	confine	9
adult	7	attach	6	code	4	confirm	7
advocate	7	attain	9	coherent	9	**conflict** (p. 53)	5
affect	2	attitude	4	coincide	9	conform	8
aggregate	6	**attribute** (p. 33)	4	collapse	10	consent	3
aid	7	author	6	colleague	10	consequent	2
albeit	10	authority	1	commence	9	considerable	3
allocate (p. 113)	6	automate	8	comment	3	consist	1
alter (p. 53)	5	available	1	commission	2	**constant** (p. 23)	3
alternative	3	**aware** (p. 43)	5	**commit** (p. 63)	4	constitute	1
ambiguous	8	behalf	9	commodity	8	constrain	3
amend	5	benefit	1	**communicate** (p. 13)	4	construct	2
analogy	9	bias	8	community	2	consult	5
analyze	1	**bond** (p. 63)	6	compatible	9	**consume** (p. 33)	2
annual	4	brief	6	compensate	3	contact	5

contemporary	8	despite	4	ensure	3	fluctuate	8
context	1	detect	8	entity	5	focus	2
contract	1	deviate	8	environment	1	format	9
contradict	8	device	9	equate	2	formula	1
contrary	7	devote	9	equip	7	forthcoming	10
contrast	4	differentiate	7	equivalent	5	found	9
contribute (p. 83)	3	dimension	4	erode	9	**foundation** (p. 73)	7
controversy	9	diminish	9	error	4	framework	3
convene	3	discrete	5	establish	1	function	1
converse	9	**discriminate** (p. 3)	6	estate	6	fund	3
convert	7	displace	8	estimate	1	**fundamental** (p. 93)	5
convince	10	**display** (p. 63)	6	ethic	9	furthermore	6
cooperate (p. 113)	6	dispose	7	**ethnic** (p. 93)	4	**gender** (p. 3)	6
coordinate	3	distinct	2	evaluate	2	generate	5
core	3	distort	9	eventual	8	**generation** (p. 3)	5
corporate	3	distribute	1	evident	1	**globe** (p. 13)	7
correspond	3	**diverse** (p. 33)	6	evolve	5	goal	4
couple	7	document	3	exceed	6	grade	7
create	1	**domain** (p. 13)	6	exclude	3	grant	4
credit	2	domestic	4	exhibit	8	guarantee	7
criteria	3	dominate	3	**expand** (p. 93)	5	**guideline** (p. 83)	8
crucial	8	draft	5	expert	6	hence	4
culture	2	drama	8	explicit	6	hierarchy	7
currency	8	**duration** (p. 23)	9	exploit	8	highlight	8
cycle	4	**dynamic** (p. 73)	7	export	1	hypothesis	4
data	1	economy	1	expose	5	**identical** (p. 103)	7
debate	4	edit	6	external	5	identify	1
decade (p. 53)	7	element	2	**extract** (p. 103)	7	ideology	7
decline (p. 53)	5	eliminate	7	**facilitate** (p. 13)	5	**ignorance** (p. 113)	6
deduce	3	emerge	4	factor	1	illustrate	3
define	1	emphasis	3	feature	2	**image** (p. 3)	5
definite	7	empirical	7	federal	6	immigrate	3
demonstrate (p. 43)	3	enable	5	fee	6	impact	2
denote	8	encounter	10	file	7	**implement** (p. 83)	4
deny	7	energy	5	final	2	implicate	4
depress	10	enforce	5	finance	1	implicit	8
derive	1	enhance	6	finite	7	imply	3
design	2	enormous	10	flexible	6	impose	4

incentive	6	investigate	4	minimal	9	parallel	4
incidence	6	invoke	10	**minimize** (p. 113)	8	parameter	4
incline	10	involve	1	minimum	6	participate	2
income	1	isolate	7	ministry	6	partner	3
incorporate	6	issue	1	minor	3	passive	9
index	6	item	2	mode	7	perceive	2
indicate	1	job	4	modify	5	percent	1
individual	1	journal	2	**monitor** (p. 93)	5	period	1
induce	8	justify	3	**motive** (p. 63)	6	persist	10
inevitable	8	label	4	mutual	9	perspective	5
infer	7	labor	1	**negate** (p. 83)	3	phase	4
infrastructure	8	layer	3	**network** (p. 53)	5	phenomenon	7
inherent	9	lecture	6	**neutral** (p. 3)	6	philosophy	3
inhibit	6	legal	1	**nevertheless** (p. 13)	6	**physical** (p. 23)	3
initial	3	legislate	1	nonetheless	10	plus	8
initiate (p. 93)	6	levy	10	norm	9	policy	1
injure	2	liberal	5	normal	2	portion	9
innovate	7	license	5	**notion** (p. 43)	5	pose	10
input	6	likewise	10	notwithstanding	10	positive	2
insert	7	link	3	nuclear	8	potential	2
insight	9	locate	3	**objective** (p. 73)	5	practitioner	8
inspect	8	**logic** (p. 43)	5	obtain	2	**precede** (p. 13)	6
instance	3	maintain	2	obvious	4	precise	5
institute (p. 93)	2	major	1	occupy	4	**predict** (p. 113)	4
instruct	6	manipulate	8	occur	1	predominant	8
integral (p. 63)	9	manual	9	odd	10	preliminary	9
integrate	4	margin	5	offset	8	presume	6
integrity	10	mature	9	**ongoing** (p. 63)	10	previous	2
intelligence	6	maximize	3	**option** (p. 43)	4	primary	2
intense	8	mechanism	4	orient	5	**prime** (p. 3)	5
interact	3	media	7	outcome	3	principal	4
intermediate	9	mediate	9	output	4	**principle** (p. 73)	1
internal	4	**medical** (p. 103)	5	overall	4	prior	4
interpret	1	medium	9	overlap	9	**priority** (p. 113)	7
interval	6	**mental** (p. 43)	5	overseas	6	proceed	1
intervene	7	method	1	panel	10	process	1
intrinsic	10	migrate	6	paradigm	7	professional	4
invest	2	military	9	paragraph	8	prohibit	7

project (p. 93)	4	respond	1	stable	5	thesis	7
promote	4	restore	8	**statistic** (p. 103)	4	topic	7
proportion	3	restrain	9	status	4	trace	6
prospect	8	restrict	2	straightforward	10	tradition	2
protocol	9	**retain** (p. 13)	4	strategy	2	transfer	2
psychology (p. 23)	5	**reveal** (p. 103)	6	**stress** (p. 73)	4	transform	6
publication	7	revenue	5	structure	1	transit	5
publish	3	reverse	7	style	5	transmit	7
purchase	2	revise	8	submit	7	transport	6
pursue	5	revolution	9	subordinate	9	trend	5
qualitative	9	rigid	9	subsequent	4	trigger	9
quote	7	role	1	subsidy	6	**ultimate** (p. 113)	7
radical	8	route	9	substitute	5	undergo	10
random	8	scenario	9	successor	7	underlie	6
range	2	schedule	8	sufficient	3	undertake	4
ratio	5	scheme	3	sum	4	uniform	8
rational (p. 23)	6	scope	6	summary	4	unify	9
react	3	section	1	supplement	9	unique	7
recover	6	sector	1	survey	2	**utilize** (p. 73)	6
refine	9	secure	2	survive	7	valid	3
regime	4	seek	2	suspend	9	vary	1
region	2	select	2	sustain	5	vehicle	8
register	3	sequence	3	**symbol** (p. 3)	5	version	5
regulate	2	series	4	tape	6	via	8
reinforce (p. 63)	8	sex	3	**target** (p. 113)	5	violate	9
reject	5	**shift** (p. 83)	3	task	3	virtual	8
relax	9	significant	1	team	9	visible	7
release	7	similar	1	technical	3	vision	9
relevant	2	simulate	7	technique	3	visual	8
reluctance	10	site	2	technology	3	volume	3
rely	3	so-called	10	temporary	9	voluntary	7
remove	3	sole	7	tense	8	welfare	5
require	1	somewhat	7	terminate	8	whereas	5
research	1	source	1	text	2	whereby	10
reside	2	specific	1	theme	8	**widespread** (p. 113)	8
resolve	4	specify	3	theory	1		
resource	2	sphere	9	thereby	8		

APPENDIX B

Affix Charts

Learning the meanings of affixes can help you identify unfamiliar words you read or hear. A *prefix* is a letter or group of letters at the beginning of a word. It usually changes the meaning. A *suffix* is a letter or group of letters at the end of a word. It usually changes the part of speech. The charts below contain common prefixes and suffixes. Refer to the charts as you use this book.

PREFIX	MEANING	EXAMPLE
a-, ab-, il-, im-, in-, ir-, un-	not, without	atypical, abnormal illegal, impossible, inconvenient, irregular, unfair
anti-	opposed to, against	antisocial, antiseptic
co-, col-, com-, con-, cor-	with, together	coexist, collect, commune, connect, correct
de-	give something the opposite quality	decriminalize
dis-	not, remove	disapprove, disarm
ex-	no longer, former	ex-wife, ex-president
ex-	out, from	export, exit
extra-	outside, beyond	extracurricular, extraordinary
in-, im-	in, into	incoming, import
inter-	between, among	international
post-	later than, after	postgraduate
pro-	in favor of	pro-education
semi-	half, partly	semicircle, semi-literate
sub-	under, below, less important	subway, submarine, subordinate
super-	larger, greater, stronger	supermarket, supervisor

SUFFIX	MEANING	EXAMPLE
-able, -ible	having the quality of, capable of *(adj)*	comfortable, responsible
-al, -ial	relating to *(adj)*	professional, ceremonial
-ence, -ance, -ency, -ancy,	the act, state, or quality of *(n)*	intelligence, performance, competency, conservancy
-ation, -tion, -ion	the act, state, or result of *(n)*	examination, selection, facilitation
-er, -or, -ar, -ist	someone who does a particular thing *(n)*	photographer, editor, beggar, psychologist
-ful	full of *(adj)*	beautiful, harmful, fearful
-ify, -ize	give something a particular quality *(v)*	clarify, modernize
-ility	the quality of *(n)*	affordability, responsibility, humility
-ism	a political or religious belief system *(n)*	atheism, capitalism
-ist	relating to (or someone who has) a political or religious belief *(adj, n)*	Buddhist, socialist
-ive, -ous, -ious,	having a particular quality *(adj)*	creative, dangerous, mysterious
-ity	a particular quality *(n)*	popularity, creativity
-less	without *(adj)*	careless, worthless
-ly	in a particular way *(adj, adv)*	briefly, fluently
-ment	conditions that result from something *(n)*	government, development
-ness	quality of *(n)*	happiness, seriousness

APPENDIX C

Student Presentation Evaluation Forms for Express Your Ideas

Use these forms to evaluate your classmates' presentations.

UNIT 1

EVALUATION FORM: Using an outline

CATEGORY		RATING	HOW TO IMPROVE	
5 = Very strong and clear	4 = Strong but with a few errors	3 = Good but some distracting errors	2 = Some sections need more work	1 = Needs a lot of improvement
DELIVERY Speaker looked at me and did not read the presentation.				
COMPREHENSIBILITY Speaker stressed syllables clearly.				
FLUENCY Speaker's rate of speech was comfortable for me.				
ORGANIZATION Speaker clearly identified the introduction, main ideas, and conclusion.				
COMPLEXITY Speaker discussed main ideas clearly and used details to explain these ideas.				

Total: _____

UNIT 2

EVALUATION FORM: Using examples

CATEGORY		RATING	HOW TO IMPROVE	
5 = Very strong and clear	4 = Strong but with a few errors	3 = Good but some distracting errors	2 = Some sections need more work	1 = Needs a lot of improvement
DELIVERY Speaker looked at me while stating at least one complete sentence.				
COMPREHENSIBILITY Speaker said important words more clearly, slowly, and with a higher pitch.				
FLUENCY Speaker sounded confident.				
ORGANIZATION Speaker identified the topic, main ideas, and examples.				
COMPLEXITY Speaker explained and clarified main ideas with examples I could understand.				

Total: _____

UNIT 3

EVALUATION FORM: Describing sensory details

CATEGORY		RATING	HOW TO IMPROVE	
5 = Very strong and clear	4 = Strong but with a few errors	3 = Good but some distracting errors	2 = Some sections need more work	1 = Needs a lot of improvement
DELIVERY Speaker showed interest in me by making eye contact often.				
COMPREHENSIBILITY Speaker used contractions.				
FLUENCY Speaker's voice showed emotion without overusing fillers (*uhs, ums*).				
ORGANIZATION Speaker used sensory details that helped me understand the main ideas.				
COMPLEXITY Speaker chose sensory details that effectively supported his or her ideas.				

Total: _____

UNIT 4

EVALUATION FORM: Developing an introduction

CATEGORY		RATING	HOW TO IMPROVE	
5 = Very strong and clear	4 = Strong but with a few errors	3 = Good but some distracting errors	2 = Some sections need more work	1 = Needs a lot of improvement
DELIVERY Speaker appeared confident by looking directly at me while presenting his or her ideas with enthusiasm.				
COMPREHENSIBILITY Speaker usually used /ə/ when saying words with unstressed vowels.				
FLUENCY Speaker sounded confident.				
ORGANIZATION Speaker gave me a list of his or her main ideas in a clear, brief introduction.				
COMPLEXITY Speaker used enough details about each VUCA Prime characteristic to convince me to accept his or her ideas.				

Total: _____

UNIT 5

EVALUATION FORM: **Moving from one point to the next**

CATEGORY	RATING	HOW TO IMPROVE	
5 = Very strong and clear 4 = Strong but with a few errors	3 = Good but some distracting errors	2 = Some sections need more work	1 = Needs a lot of improvement
DELIVERY Speaker showed enthusiasm in sharing personal information.			
COMPREHENSIBILITY Speaker pronounced -s and -ed endings clearly.			
FLUENCY Speaker used a comfortable rate of speaking without hesitating to search for vocabulary.			
ORGANIZATION Speaker used transitions to guide me to the next main idea.			
COMPLEXITY Speaker was knowledgeable about the learning strengths and how each contributes to learning.			

Total: _____

UNIT 6

EVALUATION FORM: **Concluding your presentation**

CATEGORY	RATING	HOW TO IMPROVE	
5 = Very strong and clear 4 = Strong but with a few errors	3 = Good but some distracting errors	2 = Some sections need more work	1 = Needs a lot of improvement
DELIVERY Speaker gave important dates without reading them from his or her outline.			
COMPREHENSIBILITY Speaker paused at appropriate places so I could hear dates and details clearly.			
FLUENCY Speaker gave dates and details clearly.			
ORGANIZATION Speaker helped me remember the key ideas by summarizing them clearly in a brief conclusion.			
COMPLEXITY Speaker clearly explained key details associated with each event on the timeline.			

Total: _____

UNIT 7

EVALUATION FORM: Using an attention-getting opener

CATEGORY		RATING	HOW TO IMPROVE	
5 = Very strong and clear	4 = Strong but with a few errors	3 = Good but some distracting errors	2 = Some sections need more work	1 = Needs a lot of improvement
DELIVERY Speaker spoke with enthusiasm to effectively communicate our classmate's passion.				
COMPREHENSIBILITY Speaker linked and blended sounds naturally.				
FLUENCY Speaker discussed the topic without using long or unnatural pauses.				
ORGANIZATION Speaker pulled me into his or her presentation by starting with a surprising or interesting question, statement, or quote.				
COMPLEXITY Speaker explained our classmate's motivations clearly using ideas provided in the lecture.				

Total: _____

UNIT 8

EVALUATION FORM: Presenting with visual aids

CATEGORY		RATING	HOW TO IMPROVE	
5 = Very strong and clear	4 = Strong but with a few errors	3 = Good but some distracting errors	2 = Some sections need more work	1 = Needs a lot of improvement
DELIVERY Speaker glanced quickly at visual aid and then spoke directly to me and my classmates.				
COMPREHENSIBILITY Speaker used correct intonation to signal the end of sentences and questions.				
FLUENCY Speaker gave information naturally without unnecessary pauses.				
ORGANIZATION Speaker used visual aids directly related to the ideas.				
COMPLEXITY Speaker used enough details and visuals for me to understand the ideas discussed.				

Total: _____

UNIT 9

EVALUATION FORM: Using nonverbal communication

CATEGORY		RATING	HOW TO IMPROVE	
5 = Very strong and clear	4 = Strong but with a few errors	3 = Good but some distracting errors	2 = Some sections need more work	1 = Needs a lot of improvement
DELIVERY Speaker connected with me by making eye contact and smiling to show enthusiasm.				
COMPREHENSIBILITY Speaker made the key points clear by emphasizing important words.				
FLUENCY The speaker used a smooth rate of speech.				
ORGANIZATION Speaker guided me through the presentation by using an attention-getting opener, stating the problem and proposed change, and discussing the benefits of making the change.				
COMPLEXITY Speaker presented ideas appealing to me and practical information for me to use following the presentation.				

Total: _____

UNIT 10

EVALUATION FORM: Persuading your audience

CATEGORY		RATING	HOW TO IMPROVE	
5 = Very strong and clear	4 = Strong but with a few errors	3 = Good but some distracting errors	2 = Some sections need more work	1 = Needs a lot of improvement
DELIVERY Speaker glanced quickly at outline and slides *before* starting to speak.				
COMPREHENSIBILITY Speaker helped me focus better on important ideas by reducing and contracting words.				
FLUENCY Speaker used intonation to show enthusiasm.				
ORGANIZATION Speaker discussed issues, solutions, and resulting benefits with supporting facts and ideas.				
COMPLEXITY Speaker used convincing information and visuals to influence my opinion.				

Total: _____

UNIT 11
EVALUATION FORM: Using quotations

CATEGORY		RATING	HOW TO IMPROVE	
5 = Very strong and clear	4 = Strong but with a few errors	3 = Good but some distracting errors	2 = Some sections need more work	1 = Needs a lot of improvement
DELIVERY Speakers presented information confidently by speaking with adequate volume while looking at me.				
COMPREHENSIBILITY Speakers used stress to help me focus on key words.				
FLUENCY Speakers delivered quotations without breaks or hesitations.				
ORGANIZATION Speakers took turns describing and discussing two (or more) aspects of the scientific advance.				
COMPLEXITY Speakers offered appropriate quotations and details to support their main ideas, and offered information on how the scientific advance will help us.				

Total: _____

UNIT 12
EVALUATION FORM: Answering audience questions

CATEGORY		RATING	HOW TO IMPROVE	
5 = Very strong and clear	4 = Strong but with a few errors	3 = Good but some distracting errors	2 = Some sections need more work	1 = Needs a lot of improvement
DELIVERY Speaker looked directly at me and my classmates while answering our questions.				
COMPREHENSIBILITY Speaker used pauses to signal important information.				
FLUENCY Speaker told the survivor's story without fillers.				
ORGANIZATION Speaker used a brief introduction, interesting details, and clear conclusion, and invited my questions.				
COMPLEXITY Speaker linked story details to personal learning and provided clear, comprehensive responses to questions.				

Total: _____

Unit 5 Learning Strengths Questionnaire

In each category (1–9), check (√) all statements that describe your learning.

1
- ☐ Reading an instruction manual is the best way to learn how something works.
- ☐ I keep a daily or weekly journal of my thoughts and activities.
- ☐ Learning new vocabulary is important to me.
- ☐ I enjoy playing word games.

2
- ☐ I'm very good at completing math problems.
- ☐ I enjoy doing science projects.
- ☐ Remembering telephone numbers is easy for me.
- ☐ I like trying to solve a mystery.

3
- ☐ I enjoy playing a musical instrument.
- ☐ Listening to music helps me to relax.
- ☐ I often sing or hum tunes as I work.
- ☐ I enjoy entertainment that includes music, such as concerts and musicals.

4
- ☐ I like to create things from unusual materials.
- ☐ Drawing relaxes me.
- ☐ I enjoy putting together a puzzle.
- ☐ Making things with my hands is a satisfying activity.

5
- ☐ I enjoy looking up places on maps.
- ☐ When someone gives me directions to a place, I can find it without difficulty.
- ☐ I don't get lost easily when I travel.
- ☐ I like using charts to analyze data.

6
- ☐ I learn best when I'm able to move around rather than sit still.
- ☐ I enjoy repeating activities until I can do them well.
- ☐ When I have a problem, going for a walk helps me discover how to solve it.
- ☐ I enjoy working jigsaw puzzles.

7
- ☐ Participating in a group project helps me learn.
- ☐ I like to help others learn new things.
- ☐ I enjoy organizing group activities.
- ☐ Being part of a team makes me feel important.

8
- ☐ I prefer to complete a project by myself.
- ☐ Individual sports are more interesting than team sports.
- ☐ I enjoy visiting with one friend at a time.
- ☐ My idea of a wonderful evening is quietly reading a good book.

9
- ☐ I'm interested in the environment.
- ☐ I prefer a walk in nature to a walk in the city.
- ☐ I enjoy interacting with animals.
- ☐ I'm aware of what phase the moon is in.

SCORING YOUR QUESTIONNAIRE:

Count the number of responses in each category. The numbers help to show which are your top learning strengths.

- ____ **1:** Verbal intelligence
- ____ **2:** Mathematical intelligence
- ____ **3:** Musical intelligence
- ____ **4:** Artistic intelligence
- ____ **5:** Spatial intelligence
- ____ **6:** Kinesthetic intelligence
- ____ **7:** Interpersonal intelligence
- ____ **8:** Intrapersonal intelligence
- ____ **9:** Nature intelligence

Notes and Assignments

Photo Credits